UNLOCKING HIDDEN PATTERNS: ADVANCED FEATURE ENGINEERING FOR MACHINE LEARNING

DR.P.SAVARIDASSAN
DR.M.MARANCO
DR.M.SIVAKUMAR
DR.N.KRISHNARAJ

Made with ♥ on the Notion Press Platform
www.notionpress.com

Contents

ONE
INTRODUCTION

Machine learning is a subfield of artificial intelligence that focuses on developing systems that can learn from data and improve their performance on a specific task without being explicitly programmed. It's a data-driven approach where algorithms are trained on large datasets to identify patterns, make predictions, and automate decision-making processes. In the realm of machine learning, the quality of features is paramount to unlocking hidden patterns and driving accurate predictions. Feature engineering, the art of creating or transforming raw data into meaningful features, is a critical step in building effective models. This book delves into advanced techniques for feature engineering, equipping you with the tools and knowledge to extract valuable insights from complex datasets. By mastering these techniques, you'll be able to enhance model performance, uncover hidden relationships, and make data-driven decisions with confidence.Feature engineering is the process of transforming raw data into meaningful features that can be used by machine learning algorithms. By carefully selecting and engineering features, you can improve the accuracy and interpretability of your models. This involves techniques such as data cleaning, normalization, feature selection, and feature creation. Effective feature engineering is essential for extracting valuable insights from data and building powerful machine learning models. Machine learning is a field of artificial intelligence that empowers computers to learn from data and improve their performance on a specific task without being explicitly programmed. By identifying patterns and relationships within data, machine learning algorithms can make predictions, classify information, and automate decision-making processes. Algorithms are trained on labeled data to learn a mapping function between inputs and outputs. Examples include regression and classification tasks. Algorithms learn from unlabeled data to discover patterns and structures within the data. Examples include clustering and dimensionality reduction. Algorithms learn through trial and error, receiving rewards or penalties based on their actions. Examples include game-playing and robotics. A subset of machine learning that uses artificial neural networks with multiple layers to learn complex patterns from large datasets.

This technology has revolutionized industries such as healthcare, finance, and marketing, enabling businesses to extract valuable insights from their data and gain a competitive edge. Feature engineering is the cornerstone of successful machine learning projects. By carefully selecting and transforming raw data into meaningful features, you can significantly improve the performance of your models. Effective feature engineering involves understanding the underlying domain knowledge, exploring data patterns, and applying appropriate techniques to extract valuable information. By investing time and effort into feature engineering, you can unlock the hidden potential of your data and build more accurate and interpretable models. Whether you're a seasoned data scientist or just starting your journey into machine learning, this book will provide you with the essential knowledge and skills to unlock the hidden patterns within your data.

TWO

FOUNDATIONS OF FEATURE ENGINEERING

The foundation of effective machine learning lies in the quality of your features. Feature engineering, the process of transforming raw data into meaningful representations, is a critical step in building accurate and predictive models. This section delves into the essential techniques and concepts that form the bedrock of feature engineering, providing you with a solid understanding of how to prepare your data for machine learning.Feature engineering is the process of transforming raw data into meaningful features that can be used by machine learning algorithms. It involves selecting, creating, and transforming features to improve model performance and interpretability. Understanding the characteristics of your data, including its distribution, outliers, and missing values. Cleaning and preparing data for analysis, such as handling missing values, normalization, and standardization. Identifying the most relevant features for your model, reducing dimensionality and improving efficiency. Creating new features from existing ones to capture more complex relationships and patterns. Converting categorical variables into numerical representations. Scaling numerical features to a specific range. Grouping numerical features into discrete bins. Creating new features by combining existing features. Creating features based on time-related information, such as time of day, day of week, or season. By mastering these foundational techniques, you can significantly improve the performance and interpretability of your machine learning models.

THE IMPORTANCE OF FEATURE ENGINEERING IN MACHINE LEARNING

The importance of feature engineering in machine learning cannot be overstated. Features are the building blocks of machine learning models, and their quality directly impacts the model's performance. By carefully selecting and engineering features, you can:

- **Improve model accuracy:** Well-crafted features can help models capture complex patterns and relationships within the data, leading to more accurate predictions. For example, creating interaction terms between features can reveal non-linear relationships that might otherwise be missed.
- **Reduce dimensionality:** Feature engineering can help reduce the dimensionality of your data, making it easier to train models and preventing overfitting. This can be achieved through techniques like feature selection, which identifies the most relevant features, and dimensionality reduction, which transforms data into a lower-dimensional space while preserving important information.
- **Enhance interpretability:** Meaningful features can make it easier to understand how a model is making decisions. For example, using domain-specific features can provide insights into the factors that are driving the model's predictions. This can improve transparency and accountability, especially in critical applications like healthcare and finance.
- **Avoid bias:** Poorly engineered features can introduce bias into models, leading to unfair or discriminatory outcomes. For example, using historical data that contains biases can

perpetuate those biases in the model's predictions. By carefully considering the potential biases in your data and features, you can help mitigate these risks.

In essence, feature engineering is the art of transforming raw data into information that machines can understand and use to make informed decisions. By mastering this skill, you can unlock the full potential of machine learning and build powerful models that drive real-world impact.

THE ART AND SCIENCE OF FEATURE ENGINEERING

In the world of machine learning, the quality of features is crucial to a model's success. Feature engineering, the process of creating or choosing relevant features from raw data, is a vital step that can significantly impact model performance. It's both an artistic and scientific endeavor, requiring intuition, creativity, and a deep understanding of the data and the problem at hand. While automated tools exist, human expertise is still essential for crafting features that reveal the underlying patterns and relationships within the data. This chapter explores the fundamental principles of feature engineering, focusing on the art of feature creation and the science of feature selection. By mastering these techniques, data scientists can uncover hidden insights and develop powerful machine learning models. Features are the fundamental building blocks of machine learning models. They represent the characteristics or attributes of the data that are used to train and make predictions with the model. In essence, features are the language through which the model understands and interprets the data.

Feature Engineering

The process of creating or selecting features is known as feature engineering. It's a crucial step in machine learning, as it involves transforming raw data into a form that is suitable for modeling. This often involves:

- **Feature Selection:** Choosing the most relevant features from a larger set.
- **Feature Extraction:** Creating new features from existing ones.
- **Feature Transformation:** Applying mathematical operations to features to improve their suitability for modeling.

Examples of Features

- **Image Classification:** Features might include pixel values, edge detection results, or pre-trained convolutional neural network (CNN) embeddings.
- **Natural Language Processing:** Features could be words, n-grams, or word embeddings.
- **Time Series Analysis:** Features might include lagged values, differences, or seasonal components.

In conclusion, features are the cornerstone of machine learning. By carefully selecting, creating, and transforming features, we can empower our models to learn from data and make accurate predictions.

KEY CONCEPTS AND TERMINOLOGY

Feature engineering is the process of transforming raw data into meaningful features that can be used by machine learning algorithms. Here are some key concepts and terminology related to feature engineering:

1. Data Exploration and Preprocessing

Data exploration is the initial step in the feature engineering process. It involves analyzing the data to gain a better understanding of its characteristics, distribution, and potential issues. This can be done through various techniques, such as:

- Calculating measures like mean, median, mode, standard deviation, and quartiles to get a sense of the data's distribution.
- Creating plots and charts (e.g., histograms, scatter plots, box plots) to visualize the data and identify patterns, outliers, and

trends.

- Measuring the relationships between variables to identify potential dependencies.
- Identifying and handling missing data points, which can significantly impact model performance.

Data cleaning is another essential step in feature engineering. It involves identifying and correcting errors, inconsistencies, and missing values in the data. This can be done through techniques such as:

- Filling in missing values with estimated values based on other data points or statistical methods.
- Identifying and removing data points that are significantly different from the rest of the data, which can skew the results of analysis.
- Correcting errors or inconsistencies in the data, such as typos or incorrect values.

Data normalization and data standardization are techniques used to scale numerical features to a specific range. This can be helpful for algorithms that are sensitive to the scale of features, such as gradient descent.

- Normalization: Scales features to a specific range, typically between 0 and 1. This can be done using techniques like min-max scaling or z-score normalization.
- Standardization: Centers features around 0 and scales them to have a standard deviation of 1. This is often used when the data is normally distributed.

By effectively exploring, cleaning, and preprocessing the data, you can ensure that your machine learning models are trained on high-quality data, leading to more accurate and reliable results.

2. Feature Selection and Extraction

Feature selection is the process of identifying the most relevant features for a given task, reducing dimensionality and improving model performance. This can be achieved through various methods:

Filter Methods:

- Correlation analysis: Measures the linear relationship between features and the target variable. Features with high correlation can be selected.
- Chi-squared test: Assesses the independence between categorical features and the target variable. Features with significant associations can be selected.
- ANOVA F-test: Measures the variance explained by a feature relative to the total variance in the data. Features with high F-values can be selected.

Wrapper Methods:

- Forward selection: Starts with an empty set of features and gradually adds features based on their performance in a model.
- Backward elimination: Starts with all features and gradually removes features that do not contribute significantly to model performance.
- Recursive feature elimination: Iteratively removes features that have the least impact on model performance.

Embedded Methods:

- Regularization: Penalizes complex models to prevent overfitting and encourage feature selection. Techniques like L1 regularization (Lasso) and L2 regularization (Ridge) can be used.
- Tree-based methods: Decision trees and random forests can be used to identify important features based on their information gain or impurity reduction.

Feature Extraction:

- Principal Component Analysis (PCA): Creates new features that are linear combinations of the original features, capturing the most variance in the data.
- t-SNE: A non-linear dimensionality reduction technique that preserves local structure in the data.
- Autoencoders: Neural networks that learn to encode and decode data, capturing the most important features.

By effectively selecting and extracting features, you can improve the performance of your machine learning models, reduce computational costs, and enhance model interpretability.

3. Feature Transformation

Feature transformation involves creating new features from existing ones to capture more complex relationships and improve model performance. Some common feature transformation techniques include:

One-Hot Encoding:

- Converting categorical variables (e.g., colors, countries) into numerical representations that can be used by machine learning algorithms.
- For each category, a new binary feature is created. If the category is present, the corresponding feature is set to 1; otherwise, it is set to 0.
- **Example:** If a categorical variable has three categories (red, green, blue), one-hot encoding would create three new binary features: "is_red," "is_green," and "is_blue."

Binning:

- Grouping numerical features into discrete bins to reduce the number of unique values and improve model performance.
- Divide the range of a numerical feature into a specified number of bins and assign each data point to the corresponding bin.

- **Example:** For a numerical feature representing age, you could create bins such as "0-18," "19-30," "31-45," and so on.

Interaction Terms:

- Capturing non-linear relationships between features by creating new features that are the product of existing features.
- Multiply existing features together to create new features that represent the interaction between them.
- **Example:** If you have two features, "age" and "income," you could create an interaction term "age_income" by multiplying the two features together.

Time-Based Features:

- Incorporating temporal information into your features to capture trends, seasonality, and other time-related patterns.
- Create new features based on time-related information, such as:
    - **Time of day:** Hour, minute, second
    - **Day of week:** Monday, Tuesday, ..., Sunday
    - **Month:** January, February, ..., December
    - **Year:** 2023, 2024, ...
    - **Time-based differences:** Calculate differences between time-related features (e.g., time elapsed since a specific event).

By effectively using these feature transformation techniques, you can enhance the predictive power of your machine learning models and gain valuable insights from your data.

4.Feature Scaling

Feature scaling is a crucial preprocessing step in machine learning that involves transforming numerical features to a consistent range. This helps ensure that different features are treated fairly by the algorithm, preventing features with larger magnitudes from dominating the learning process.

Normalization:

Scales features to a specific range, typically between 0 and 1.

Methods:

- **Min-max scaling:** Scales features to a specific range (e.g., 0 to 1) using the minimum and maximum values of the feature.
- **Robust scaling:** Scales features using the interquartile range (IQR) to make it less sensitive to outliers.

Standardization:

- Centers features around 0 and scales them to have a standard deviation of 1.
- Subtracts the mean from each feature and divides by the standard deviation.

Choosing the right scaling method depends on the characteristics of your data and the algorithm you are using. For example, normalization is often used when the data is bounded, while standardization is more suitable for normally distributed data. By applying appropriate feature scaling techniques, you can improve the convergence speed of your machine learning algorithms, enhance model performance, and make your models more interpretable.

5. Feature Evaluation

Feature evaluation is the process of assessing the relevance and importance of features in a machine learning model. This helps identify the most informative features and can improve model performance and interpretability.

Correlation Analysis:

Measures the linear relationship between features and the target variable.

Methods:

- **Pearson correlation:** Measures the linear relationship between two continuous variables.
- **Spearman correlation:** Measures the monotonic relationship between two variables, regardless of their linearity.
- **Kendall correlation:** Measures the rank-based correlation between two variables.

High correlation between a feature and the target variable suggests that the feature is likely to be informative for the model. However, it's important to note that correlation does not imply causation, and highly correlated features may contain redundant information.

Feature Importance:

Assessing the relative importance of features in a machine learning model.

Methods:

- **Permutation importance:** Randomly shuffling the values of a feature and measuring the impact on model performance.
- **Mean decrease impurity:** Measuring the average decrease in impurity (e.g., Gini impurity, entropy) that a feature contributes to a decision tree or random forest model.
- **Coefficient magnitudes:** In linear models, the magnitude of the coefficients associated with each feature can indicate its importance.

The correlation between features and the target variable and assessing their relative importance, you can identify the most informative features and focus your efforts on feature engineering and model building. By understanding these key concepts and terminology, you can effectively apply feature engineering techniques to improve the performance of your machine learning models.

THE FEATURE ENGINEERING PIPELINE

The feature engineering pipeline is a systematic approach to transforming raw data into meaningful features that can be used by machine learning algorithms. It typically involves the following steps:

1. Data Exploration and Preprocessing:

Data exploration is the initial step in the feature engineering process. It involves analyzing the data to gain a better understanding of its characteristics, distribution, and potential issues. This can be done through various techniques, such as:

- Summary statistics: Calculating measures like mean, median, mode, standard deviation, and quartiles to get a sense of the data's distribution.
- Visualization: Creating plots and charts (e.g., histograms, scatter plots, box plots) to visualize the data and identify patterns, outliers, and trends.
- Correlation analysis: Measuring the relationships between variables to identify potential dependencies.
- Missing value analysis: Identifying and handling missing data points, which can significantly impact model performance.

Data cleaning is another essential step in feature engineering. It involves identifying and correcting errors, inconsistencies, and missing values in the data. This can be done through techniques such as:

- Imputation: Filling in missing values with estimated values based on other data points or statistical methods.
- Outlier detection and removal: Identifying and removing data points that are significantly different from the rest of the data, which can skew the results of analysis.
- Data correction: Correcting errors or inconsistencies in the data, such as typos or incorrect values.

Data normalization and data standardization are techniques used to scale numerical features to a specific range. This can be helpful for algorithms that are sensitive to the scale of features, such as gradient descent.

- Normalization: Scales features to a specific range, typically between 0 and 1. This can be done using techniques like min-max scaling or z-score normalization.
- Standardization: Centers features around 0 and scales them to have a standard deviation of 1. This is often used when the data is normally distributed.

By effectively exploring, cleaning, and preprocessing the data, you can ensure that your machine learning models are trained on high-quality data, leading to more accurate and reliable results.

2. Feature Selection:

Feature selection is the process of identifying the most relevant features for a given task, reducing dimensionality and improving model performance. This can be achieved through various methods:

Filter Methods:

- Correlation analysis: Measures the linear relationship between features and the target variable. Features with high correlation can be selected.
- Chi-squared test: Assesses the independence between categorical features and the target variable. Features with significant associations can be selected.
- ANOVA F-test: Measures the variance explained by a feature relative to the total variance in the data. Features with high F-values can be selected.

Wrapper Methods:

- Forward selection: Starts with an empty set of features and gradually adds features based on their performance in a machine learning model.

- Backward elimination: Starts with all features and gradually removes features that do not contribute significantly to model performance.
- Recursive feature elimination: Iteratively removes features that have the least impact on model performance.

Embedded Methods:

- Regularization: Penalizes complex models to prevent overfitting and encourage feature selection. Techniques like L1 regularization (Lasso) and L2 regularization (Ridge) can be used.
- Tree-based methods: Decision trees and random forests can be used to identify important features based on their information gain or impurity reduction.

By effectively selecting features, you can reduce the dimensionality of your data, improve model interpretability, and potentially enhance model performance. However, it's important to note that the best feature selection methodmay vary depending on the specific dataset and machine learning task.

3. Feature Creation:

- One-hot encoding: Converting categorical variables into numerical representations.
- Binning: Grouping numerical features into discrete bins.
- Interaction terms: Creating new features by combining existing features.
- Time-based features: Creating features based on time-related information.

4. Feature Scaling:

- Normalization: Scaling features to a specific range (e.g., 0 to 1).

- Standardization: Centering and scaling features to have a mean of 0 and a standard deviation of 1.

5. Feature Evaluation:

- Correlation analysis: Measuring the relationship between features and the target variable.
- Feature importance: Assessing the relative importance of features in a machine learning model.

By following this pipeline, you can ensure that your machine learning models are trained on high-quality features, leading to improved performance and interpretability. It's important to note that the specific steps and techniques used in the feature engineering pipeline may vary depending on the nature of the data and the machine learning task at hand.

KEY CONSIDERATIONS AND BEST PRACTICES IN FEATURE ENGINEERING

Domain Knowledge

Incorporating insights from domain experts can lead to the creation of features that are more informative and relevant to the specific problem.

Understanding the underlying domain helps identify key factors and relationships that might not be immediately apparent from the data alone.

Data Quality

Ensuring that the data is correct and free from errors is essential for reliable feature engineering.

Missing data can hinder feature creation and model performance. Imputation techniques can be used to fill in missing values.

Inconsistent data can introduce noise and bias. Data cleaning and standardization can help address inconsistencies.

Feature Relevance

Choosing features that have a strong relationship with the target variable can improve model performance.

Methods like feature importance scores, correlation analysis, and recursive feature elimination can help identify relevant features.

Feature Engineering Techniques

Exploring a variety of techniques can help you find the best approach for your specific data and problem.

Different techniques may be more suitable for different types of data (e.g., numerical, categorical, text).

Feature Interaction

Understanding how features interact with each other can help create more informative features.

New features can be created by combining existing features to capture interactions.

Feature Scaling

Scaling features to a common range can improve the convergence of optimization algorithms and prevent features with large magnitudes from dominating the learning process.

Common scaling techniques include normalization (scaling to a range of 0 to 1) and standardization (centering and scaling to a unit variance).

Feature Regularization

Regularization techniques like L1 and L2 regularization can help prevent models from overfitting by penalizing complex models.

Regularization can help strike a balance between underfitting and overfitting.

Iterative Process

Feature engineering is often an iterative process, allowing for continuous refinement and improvement.

Experiment with different feature engineering techniques and evaluate their impact on model performance.

By carefully considering these factors and applying best practices, you can effectively engineer features that enhance your machine learning models and improve their predictive power.

THREE

FEATURE TYPES AND REPRESENTATIONS

In the realm of machine learning, the quality and relevance of features play a pivotal role in determining a model's performance. Features are the fundamental building blocks that represent the characteristics or attributes of data, enabling models to learn patterns and make predictions. Understanding the different types of features and how they can be represented is essential for effective feature engineering and model development. This chapter delves into the intricacies of feature types, exploring numerical, categorical, and textual features, and discusses the various techniques used to represent these features in a format that is suitable for machine learning algorithms. By mastering the concepts presented in this chapter, you will gain a solid foundation for crafting informative and effective features, ultimately enhancing the capabilities of your machine learning models.

NUMERICAL ,CATEGORICAL AND TEXTUAL FEATURES

Understanding Different Feature Types

In machine learning, features are the individual characteristics or attributes that describe the data. Understanding the different types of features is essential for effective feature engineering and model development. Here are the three primary feature types:

Numerical Features

Continuous:

- Examples: Age, temperature, income, height, weight, time
- Characteristics: Can take any real number value within a specific range.
- Visualization: Often represented using histograms, box plots, or scatter plots.

Discrete:

- Examples: Number of items in a cart, number of stars given in a rating, number of customers, number of products sold
- Characteristics: Can only take specific values, often integers.
- Visualization: Often represented using bar charts or pie charts.

Categorical Features

Nominal:

- Examples: Colors (red, blue, green), countries (USA, Canada, France), product types (electronics, clothing, furniture)
- Characteristics: Categories have no inherent order or ranking.
- Encoding: Often encoded using one-hot encoding or label encoding.

Ordinal:

- Examples: Educational levels (high school, bachelor's, master's), customer satisfaction ratings (very unsatisfied, unsatisfied, neutral, satisfied, very satisfied), product quality rankings (low, medium, high)
- Characteristics: Categories have an inherent order or ranking.

- Encoding: Often encoded using label encoding or ordinal encoding.

Textual Features

Representations:

- **Bag-of-Words:**
  - Each document is represented as a numerical vector where each element corresponds to the frequency of a word in the document.
  - Ignores word order and context.
  - Suitable for simple text classification tasks.
- **TF-IDF (Term Frequency-Inverse Document Frequency):**
  - Weights words based on their frequency within a document and their importance across the entire corpus.
  - Helps to address the issue of common words that may not be as informative.
- **Word Embeddings:**
  - Represent words as dense vectors in a continuous space, capturing semantic relationships between words.
  - Techniques like Word2Vec, GloVe, and FastText can be used to create word embeddings.
  - Provide a more nuanced representation of text, capturing context and semantic meaning.

Choosing the right representation for textual data depends on the specific task and the complexity of the language. For simple tasks like document classification, bag-of-words or TF-IDF might suffice. However, for more complex tasks that require understanding semantic relationships, word embeddings are often preferred.

Common Challenges and Considerations

Numerical Features

Outliers:

- Impact: Extreme values can significantly skew the data distribution, leading to biased models and inaccurate predictions.
- Identification: Outliers can be identified using techniques like statistical methods (e.g., Z-score, IQR), visualization (e.g., box plots), or domain knowledge.
- Handling: Once identified, outliers can be handled in various ways, such as removing them, capping them, or transforming them.

Scaling:

- Importance: Features with different scales can have unequal influence on the model, potentially leading to biased results.
- Techniques: Normalization (scaling to a range of 0-1) and standardization (centering and scaling to a unit variance) are common scaling techniques.
- Choosing the right technique: The choice of scaling technique depends on the specific data and model. For example, normalization is often used for algorithms that are sensitive to feature scales, while standardization is more suitable for many machine learning algorithms.

Categorical Features

Encoding:

- Necessity: Most machine learning algorithms require numerical features. Categorical features must be encoded into numerical representations.
- **Techniques:**

- One-hot encoding: Each category is represented as a binary vector. Suitable for nominal features.
- Label encoding: Categories are assigned unique integer labels. Suitable for ordinal features.
- Target encoding: Categories are replaced with the mean or median of the target variable for that category. Can be effective for high-cardinality features.

Cardinality:

- High-cardinality features: Features with a large number of unique categories can introduce dimensionality issues, leading to potential overfitting and computational challenges.
- Addressing dimensionality: Techniques like feature hashing or feature embedding can help reduce dimensionality while preserving the information in high-cardinality features.

Textual Features

Noise:

- Types of noise: Textual data can contain noise such as typos, stop words (common words like "the," "and," "a"), and inconsistencies.
- Cleaning: Preprocessing techniques like stemming (reducing words to their root form), lemmatization (converting words to their base form), and stop word removal can help clean the data and improve model performance.

Sparsity:

- Sparse representations: Textual data often results in sparse representations, where most elements in the feature vectors are zero.
- Addressing sparsity: Techniques like dimensionality reduction (e.g., PCA, SVD) or feature selection can help reduce the dimensionality of the feature space and improve model

efficiency.

Understanding the different feature types and their associated challenges is essential for effective feature engineering. By addressing these challenges and selecting appropriate representation techniques, you can create high-quality features that enhance the performance of your machine learning models.

FEATURE TRANSFORMATIONS AND NORMALIZATION

In the realm of machine learning, the quality of features significantly impacts a model's performance. Feature transformations and normalization are essential techniques to ensure that data is presented in a format that is suitable for modeling. These methods help to improve model convergence, prevent bias, and enhance the interpretability of results. This chapter delves into the intricacies of feature transformations and normalization, exploring their importance, common techniques, and best practices for application. By understanding and effectively applying these techniques, you can optimize your machine learning models and extract valuable insights from your data.

Techniques to Improve Feature Quality and Compatibility

Feature transformations and normalization are essential techniques for preparing data for machine learning models. They help to improve feature quality and compatibility, ensuring that the data is in a suitable format for modeling.

Feature transformations involve applying mathematical operations to features to modify their distribution or create new features. Common transformations include:

Scaling, Binning, and One-Hot Encoding

Scaling:

Scaling is often necessary for algorithms that are sensitive to feature magnitudes, such as gradient descent.

The choice of scaling technique depends on the specific data and model. For example, min-max scaling is suitable for algorithms that require features to be in a specific range, while Z-score standardization is more commonly used for many machine learning algorithms.

- **Min-max scaling:** Scales features to a range of 0-1.
    - Formula: scaled_feature = (feature - min_feature) / (max_feature - min_feature)
- **Z-score standardization:** Centers features around the mean and scales them to a unit variance.
    - Formula: scaled_feature= (feature - mean_feature) / std_dev_feature
- **Robust scaling:** Uses the median and interquartile range instead of the mean and standard deviation.
    - Less sensitive to outliers.

Binning:

Binning involves grouping continuous features into discrete bins. Binning can help to handle outliers, reduce noise, and improve model interpretability. The choice of bin size is important. Too few bins can lead to loss of information, while too many bins can introduce noise.

Converting continuous features to categorical: Groups continuous features into discrete bins.

- Benefits:
    - Handles outliers
    - Reduces noise
    - Improves model interpretability
- Bin size: The choice of bin size is important. Too few bins can lead to loss of information, while too many bins can introduce

noise.

One-Hot Encoding:

One-hot encoding creates a new binary feature for each category, with a value of 1 for the corresponding category and 0 for others. One-hot encoding is suitable for nominal features that have no inherent order. One-hot encoding can increase the dimensionality of the data, especially for high-cardinality features.

- Encoding categorical features: Creates a new binary feature for each category.
- Suitable for nominal features: Has no inherent order.
- High dimensionality: Can increase the dimensionality of the data.

Feature Transformations

Log transformations:

- Used for skewed data: Transforms skewed data into a more normal distribution.
- Common use cases: For features with a long tail distribution, such as income or population.
- Formula: transformed_feature = log(feature)

Box-Cox transformations:

- Family of transformations: A family of transformations that can be used to normalize data with different shapes.
- Common use cases: For data with different levels of skewness.
- Formula: transformed_feature = (feature^lambda - 1) / lambda (for lambda != 0)

Polynomial features:

- Creating new features: Creates new features by raising existing features to powers.
- Capturing non-linear relationships: Can capture non-linear relationships between features and the target variable.
- **Example:** For a feature x, polynomial features of degree 2 would be x, x^2.

Interaction features:

- Creating new features: Creates new features by multiplying or dividing existing features.
- Capturing interactions: Can capture interactions between features that might not be apparent when considering them individually.
- **Example:** For features x1 and x2, an interaction feature would be x1 * x2.

By carefully selecting and applying feature transformations and normalization techniques, you can improve the quality and compatibility of your data, leading to better model performance and interpretability.

FOUR

FEATURE SELECTION AND EXTRACTION

In the realm of machine learning, the quality and quantity of features significantly impact a model's performance. Feature selection and extraction are essential techniques that optimize the feature space, enhancing model accuracy, interpretability, and computational efficiency.This chapter delves into the intricacies of these processes, exploring the art of selecting the most relevant features and the science of extracting new, informative features from existing data. By mastering feature selection and extraction, you can unlock hidden patterns, improve model generalization, and gain valuable insights from your data. These data features (whether you have synthetic data sets, work with big data, have missing data gaps, labeled training data, etc.) will shape the model's algorithmic abilities to learn and in consequence, it is therefore critical to analyse and pre-process datasets before application to ensure data quality. For machine learning projects, engineers must first assess all the data they have available, and answer the question 'how much data do I need?'. The analysis of a dataset should produce key insights into the data quality and quantity, as well as its distribution. Beyond this, long-term operation input data may also dynamically change with time. There are no guarantees that a user's data type or format will stay constant.

In the real-world application of machine learning, it is far from uncommon for datasets to diverge away from the picture-perfect data a machine learning model has been trained on. Determining the optimal data quantity requires a series of logical considerations and decisions, such as dropping unnecessary data, augmenting existing data, and collecting new data. A well-trained machine learning model should be exposed to a diverse range of data points. This ensures that the model can generalize well to new inputs and avoid overfitting. In essence, the dataset should contain enough information to represent the real-world scenarios the model will encounter. Understanding the model's key functionality is crucial. Different machine learning tasks (e.g., classification, regression) have varying data requirements. The complexity of the problem, the diversity of the training data, and the algorithm used all influence the necessary data quantity.

By understanding these relationships, we can gain insights into the overfitting and underfitting phenomena. Overfitting occurs when a model learns the training data too well, leading to poor generalization. Underfitting occurs when a model fails to capture the underlying patterns in the data. Striking the right balance between these two extremes is essential for building effective machine learning models.

FILTER , WRAPPER , AND EMBEDDED METHODS

Feature Selection Methods

Feature selection is a crucial step in machine learning, aimed at identifying the most relevant features that contribute significantly to model performance. By selecting a subset of features, we can reduce dimensionality, improve model interpretability, and potentially enhance generalization.

1. Filter Methods

Filter methods are a class of feature selection techniques that evaluate features independently of the machine learning model.

They rely on statistical metrics to assess the relevance of features to the target variable.

Correlation Analysis

- Correlation analysis calculates the Pearson correlation coefficient to quantify the linear relationship between two variables.
- Values: The correlation coefficient ranges from -1 to 1:
  - -1 indicates a perfect negative correlation (as one variable increases, the other decreases).
  - 0 indicates no correlation.
  - 1 indicates a perfect positive correlation (as one variable increases, the other also increases).
- Limitations: Correlation does not imply causation, and it may not capture non-linear relationships.

Chi-Squared Test

- Tests independence: For categorical features, the chi-squared test determines if there is a significant association between a feature and the target variable.
- Null hypothesis: The null hypothesis is that the feature and the target variable are independent.
- P-value: A low p-value suggests that the null hypothesis can be rejected, indicating a significant association.

ANOVA (Analysis of Variance)

- Compares means: ANOVA tests whether the means of the target variable differ significantly across different categories of a feature.
- F-statistic: The F-statistic measures the ratio of the variance between groups to the variance within groups.

- P-value: A low p-value indicates that the means are significantly different.

Pros of Filter Methods:

- Computational efficiency: Filter methods are generally fast and computationally efficient, making them suitable for large datasets.
- Simplicity: They are easy to understand and implement.

Cons of Filter Methods:

- Sensitivity to noise and outliers: Filter methods can be sensitive to noise and outliers in the data.
- Inability to capture non-linear relationships: They may not capture complex relationships between features and the target variable.
- Independence assumption: Filter methods assume that features are independent, which may not always be true in real-world data.

Despite these limitations, filter methods can be a valuable tool for feature selection, especially as a preliminary step to reduce the dimensionality of the data before using more complex methods.

2. Wrapper Methods

Wrapper methods are a class of feature selection techniques that evaluate feature subsets based on their impact on a machine learning model's performance. Unlike filter methods, wrapper methods directly consider the interaction between features and the specific model being used.

Common Wrapper Methods

Forward Selection:

- Starting point: Begins with an empty set of features.

- Iterative process: Adds one feature at a time to the set, selecting the feature that results in the greatest improvement in model performance.
- Evaluation: The performance of the model is evaluated using a chosen metric (e.g., accuracy, F1-score, RMSE).
- Termination: The process continues until a desired number of features is reached or there is no significant improvement in performance.

Backward Elimination:

- Starting point: Begins with all features.
- Iterative process: Removes one feature at a time, selecting the feature that has the least impact on model performance.
- Evaluation: The performance of the model is evaluated using a chosen metric.
- Termination: The process continues until a desired number of features is reached or there is a significant drop in performance.

Recursive Feature Elimination (RFE):

- Ranking: Ranks features based on their importance using a machine learning model.
- Elimination: Iteratively removes the least important feature until a desired number of features remains.
- Model retraining: The model is retrained with the remaining features in each iteration.

Pros and Cons of Wrapper Methods

Pros:

- Consider feature interactions: Wrapper methods explicitly consider the interaction between features and the specific model being used, which can lead to more accurate feature selection.

- Tailored to the model: They are tailored to the chosen machine learning algorithm, ensuring that the selected features are most relevant for that particular model.

Cons:

- Computational expense: Wrapper methods can be computationally expensive, especially for large datasets and complex models.
- Risk of overfitting: If not carefully controlled, wrapper methods can overfit to the training data, leading to poor generalization.

Choosing the right wrapper method depends on the specific dataset, problem, and model. For smaller datasets and simpler models, forward selection or backward elimination may be sufficient. For larger datasets and more complex models, RFE can be a more efficient option.

3. Embedded methods

Embedded methods are a class of feature selection techniques that are integrated directly into the machine learning algorithm itself. They select features during the model training process, often as a byproduct of the learning algorithm.

Common Embedded Methods

Regularization:

- **L1 (Lasso) regularization:** Adds a penalty term to the loss function that is proportional to the absolute value of the feature coefficients. This encourages sparsity, meaning that some coefficients may be set to zero, effectively removing the corresponding features from the model.
- **L2 (Ridge) regularization:** Adds a penalty term to the loss function that is proportional to the square of the feature coefficients. This reduces the magnitude of all coefficients, but does not set any to zero.

Decision Trees:

- **Feature importance:** Decision trees can provide a measure of feature importance based on their contribution to the splitting of nodes in the tree. Features that are used more frequently at higher levels of the tree are generally considered more important.

Random Forests:

- **Feature importance:** Random forests, an ensemble of decision trees, can calculate the average feature importance across all trees in the forest. Features that are used more frequently in the decision trees are considered more important.

Pros and Cons of Embedded Methods

Pros:

- **Efficiency:** Embedded methods are often more efficient than wrapper methods, as they do not require multiple rounds of model training and evaluation.
- **Good results:** Embedded methods can provide good results, especially when the algorithm is well-suited to the problem at hand.

Cons:

- **Sensitivity to algorithm choice:** The choice of algorithm can affect the feature importance scores and the effectiveness of the feature selection process.
- **Hyperparameter tuning:** Embedded methods may require careful tuning of hyperparameters, such as the regularization parameter in L1 or L2 regularization.

Choosing the Right Method

The choice of feature selection method depends on the specific dataset, problem, and model. In many cases, a combination of methods can be used to achieve the best results. By carefully selecting features, you can improve model performance, interpretability, and computational efficiency.

DIMENSIONALITY REDUCTION TECHNIQUES

Machine learning, dealing with high-dimensional data can pose significant challenges. The curse of dimensionality refers to the phenomenon where the number of features grows exponentially, leading to increased computational complexity, overfitting, and reduced model performance. Dimensionality reduction techniques offer a powerful solution by transforming high-dimensional data into a lower-dimensional space while preserving essential information. This chapter delves into the intricacies of dimensionality reduction, exploring various techniques, their underlying principles, and their applications in real-world scenarios. By mastering dimensionality reduction, you can enhance model efficiency, improve interpretability, and unlock valuable insights from complex datasets.

Dimensionality reduction techniques are essential tools for dealing with high-dimensional data. By reducing the number of features, these techniques can improve model performance, reduce computational complexity, and enhance interpretability.

Techniques to Reduce the Number of Features

Dimensionality Reduction Techniques

Principal Component Analysis (PCA)

- **Identifies principal components**: PCA finds the most important directions in the data, known as principal components, that capture the maximum variance. These components are orthogonal to each other.
- **Projects data onto a lower-dimensional space:** PCA projects the data onto a subspace defined by the principal components. This reduces the dimensionality of the data while preserving the most important information.

- **Preserves variance:** PCA aims to preserve as much variance as possible in the data when projecting it onto the lower-dimensional space.

t-Distributed Stochastic Neighbor Embedding (t-SNE)

- **Non-linear technique:** t-SNE is a non-linear dimensionality reduction technique, meaning it can capture complex relationships between data points that are not linearly separable.
- **Preserves local structure:** t-SNE preserves the local structure of the data, meaning points that are close together in the high-dimensional space tend to be close together in the low-dimensional space.
- **Visualization:** t-SNE is particularly well-suited for visualizing high-dimensional data in two or three dimensions, making it a valuable tool for exploratory data analysis.

Linear Discriminant Analysis (LDA)

- **Supervised technique:** LDA is a supervised dimensionality reduction technique, meaning it takes into account the class labels of the data points.
- **Maximizes separation:** LDA projects data onto a subspace that maximizes the separation between classes. This makes it effective for classification problems.
- **Class-specific projections:** LDA finds a projection that maximizes the between-class variance while minimizing the within-class variance.

Choosing the right dimensionality reduction technique depends on the specific dataset, problem, and desired outcome. PCA is a good choice for general-purpose dimensionality reduction, while t-SNE is excellent for visualizing high-dimensional data. LDA is particularly effective for classification problems where maximizing class separation is important.

Factor Analysis

- **Latent factors:** Factor analysis identifies underlying latent factors that explain the observed data. These factors are unobserved variables that are assumed to influence the observed variables.
- **Dimensionality reduction:** Factor analysis can be used to reduce the dimensionality of the data by representing the observed variables as linear combinations of a smaller number of latent factors.
- **Feature extraction:** The latent factors can also be interpreted as meaningful features that capture the underlying structure of the data.

Autoencoders

- **Neural networks:** Autoencoders are neural networks trained to reconstruct input data. They typically consist of an encoder and a decoder.
- **Dimensionality reduction:** The bottleneck layer of the autoencoder, which has a smaller dimensionality than the input or output layers, can be used for dimensionality reduction.
- **Learning latent representations:** The autoencoder learns to compress the input data into a lower-dimensional latent representation and then reconstruct the original data from this representation.
- **Applications:** Autoencoders have a wide range of applications, including denoising, anomaly detection, and image compression.

Choosing the right dimensionality reduction technique depends on the specific dataset, problem, and desired outcome. Factor analysis is well-suited for identifying underlying latent factors and extracting meaningful features. Autoencoders are versatile and can be used for both dimensionality reduction and other tasks.

The choice of dimensionality reduction technique depends on several factors, including:

Choosing the Right Dimensionality Reduction Technique

Linearity vs. Non-Linearity

- PCA: Well-suited for linearly related data.
- t-SNE and Autoencoders: More suitable for non-linear relationships, capturing complex patterns in the data.

Supervised vs. Unsupervised Learning

- LDA: A supervised technique, effective for classification problems where class labels are available.
- PCA and t-SNE: Unsupervised techniques, suitable for general-purpose dimensionality reduction without considering class labels.

Preservation of Local Structure

- t-SNE: Preserves local structure in the data, making it suitable for tasks where preserving relationships between nearby data points is important.

Other Considerations

- Computational cost: Some techniques, like t-SNE, can be computationally expensive for large datasets.
- Interpretability: The choice of technique may also depend on the desired level of interpretability. PCA, for example, provides a linear combination of features, which can be easier to interpret than the results from some non-linear techniques.
- Domain knowledge: Understanding the domain and the underlying relationships in the data can help guide the choice of technique.

By carefully considering these factors and applying appropriate dimensionality reduction techniques, you can effectively reduce the number of features in your data while preserving important information and improving model performance

FIVE

ADAVANCED FEATURE ENGINEERING TECHNIQUE

The quality and relevance of features significantly impact a model's performance. While basic feature engineering techniques are essential, advanced methodologies offer a powerful arsenal for extracting deeper insights and enhancing predictive accuracy. This chapter delves into the intricacies of advanced feature engineering, exploring techniques that go beyond the conventional. By mastering these techniques, you can unlock hidden patterns, optimize model performance, and gain a competitive edge in the field of machine learning.

Advanced feature engineering techniques go beyond basic preprocessing and involve creating new features or transforming existing ones to better capture the underlying patterns and relationships in the data. These techniques can significantly improve model performance, especially for complex problems.

Key Techniques

1. Feature Interaction:

Polynomial Features: Creating new features by raising existing features to powers (e.g., x^2, x^3).

Interaction Terms: Multiplying or dividing existing features to capture non-linear relationships.

2. Time Series Features:

Lagged Features: Creating features based on past values of a time series (e.g., x(t-1), x(t-2)).

Rolling Statistics: Calculating statistics (e.g., mean, standard deviation) over a window of time.

Differencing: Taking the difference between consecutive values to capture trends and seasonality.

3. Text and Natural Language Processing (NLP):

Word Embeddings: Representing words as dense vectors in a continuous space, capturing semantic relationships.

Document Embeddings: Representing entire documents as vectors, capturing the overall meaning and context.

4. Image and Computer Vision:

Convolutional Neural Networks (CNNs): Extracting features from images using convolutional layers.

Transfer Learning: Using pre-trained CNN models as feature extractors.

5. Domain-Specific Features:

Leveraging domain knowledge: Creating features that are specific to the problem domain.

Custom transformations: Applying transformations tailored to the unique characteristics of the data.

6. Feature Selection and Extraction:

Advanced techniques: Using techniques like recursive feature elimination (RFE), group lasso, and feature importance scores from tree-based models.

Benefits of Advanced Feature Engineering

- **Improved model performance:** Advanced features can capture complex relationships and patterns in the data, leading to better model accuracy.

- **Enhanced interpretability:** Well-crafted features can make models more interpretable, providing insights into how they make decisions.
- **Reduced dimensionality:** Feature engineering can help reduce the dimensionality of the data, improving computational efficiency and preventing overfitting.

By mastering advanced feature engineering techniques, you can unlock the full potential of your machine learning models and achieve exceptional results.

SIX

TEXT AND NATURAL LANGUAGE PROCESSING

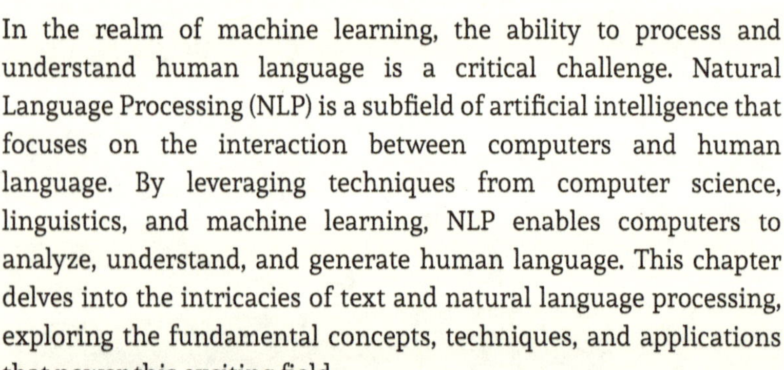

In the realm of machine learning, the ability to process and understand human language is a critical challenge. Natural Language Processing (NLP) is a subfield of artificial intelligence that focuses on the interaction between computers and human language. By leveraging techniques from computer science, linguistics, and machine learning, NLP enables computers to analyze, understand, and generate human language. This chapter delves into the intricacies of text and natural language processing, exploring the fundamental concepts, techniques, and applications that power this exciting field.

TEXT PREPROCESSING AND TOKENIZATION

Text preprocessing is the initial step in preparing textual data for analysis in natural language processing (NLP). It involves cleaning and transforming the text to remove noise and inconsistencies, making it suitable for further processing.

1. Text Preprocessing: Cleaning and Preparing Text Data

Removing Noise:

- HTML tags: Removing HTML tags can be necessary when dealing with text extracted from web pages.
- Punctuation marks: Depending on the NLP task, punctuation marks may be removed or retained. For example, in sentiment analysis, punctuation marks can provide clues about the emotional tone of the text.
- Special symbols: Removing special symbols like emojis or control characters can help to standardize the text.

Handling Contractions:

- Improving accuracy: Expanding contractions can improve the accuracy of NLP models, especially for tasks like sentiment analysis or question answering.
- Using regular expressions: Regular expressions can be used to identify and replace contractions with their expanded forms.

Correcting Typos and Errors:

- Spell checking: Using spell checking algorithms to identify and correct misspelled words.
- Grammar checking: Identifying and correcting grammatical errors.
- Contextual understanding: Consider the context of the text to ensure that corrections are accurate and meaningful.

Normalizing Text:

- Consistency: Converting text to a consistent format (e.g., lowercase) can simplify subsequent processing steps.
- Case folding: Converting all text to lowercase or uppercase can be useful for tasks that are insensitive to case.

Removing Stop Words:

- Reducing dimensionality: Removing stop words can reduce the dimensionality of the feature space, leading to more efficient models.
- Improving performance: In some cases, removing stop words can improve model performance, especially for tasks that focus on the most important words in the text.

The specific preprocessing steps required will depend on the NLP task and the characteristics of the data. It is often necessary to experiment with different preprocessing techniques to find the best approach for a given problem.

2. Tokenization Techniques

Tokenization is the process of breaking down text into smaller units called tokens. These tokens can be words, characters, or n-grams.

Word Tokenization

- Word tokenization is the most common technique, where the text is split into individual words based on spaces or punctuation marks.
- **Example:** The sentence "I love natural language processing" would be tokenized as: "I," "love," "natural," "language," "processing."
- **Considerations:** Word tokenization can be challenging in languages with complex morphology or irregular word boundaries.

Character Tokenization

- Breaking text into individual characters: Character tokenization splits the text into individual characters, regardless of word boundaries.

- Applications: Useful for tasks like character-level language modeling or spell checking.
- **Example:** The sentence "I love natural language processing" would be tokenized as: "I," "l", "o", "v", "e", " ", "n", "a", "t", "u", "r", "a", "l", " ", "l", "a", "n", "g", "u", "a", "g", "e", " ", "p", "r", "o", "c", "e", "s", "s", "i", "n", "g".

n-gram Tokenization

- Sequences of words or characters: n-gram tokenization creates sequences of n consecutive words or characters.
- **Examples:**
    - Bigrams (n=2): "I love," "love natural," "natural language"
    - Trigrams (n=3): "I love natural," "love natural language," "natural language processing"
- **Applications:** n-grams can be useful for tasks like language modeling, machine translation, and information retrieval.

Choosing the Appropriate Tokenization Technique

The choice of tokenization technique depends on the specific NLP task and the characteristics of the data. Here are some factors to consider:

- Language: Some languages have more complex morphology or irregular word boundaries, which may require different tokenization techniques.
- Task: The specific NLP task can influence the choice of tokenization technique. For example, word tokenization is often suitable for tasks like sentiment analysis or text classification, while character tokenization can be useful for tasks like spell checking or machine translation.
- Data characteristics: The characteristics of the data, such as the length of the text and the complexity of the language, can also

impact the choice of tokenization technique.

By effectively preprocessing and tokenizing text data, you can ensure that your NLP models have a clean and structured input, leading to improved performance and accuracy.

WORD EMBEDDINGS AND DOCUMENTS REPRESENTATIONS

In the realm of natural language processing (NLP), representing text data in a numerical format that can be processed by machine learning algorithms is essential. Word embeddings provide a powerful technique for capturing the semantic meaning and relationships between words, enabling machines to understand and analyze human language. This chapter delves into the intricacies of word embeddings and document representations, exploring their significance, common techniques, and applications in various NLP tasks. By mastering these concepts, you can unlock the full potential of your NLP models and achieve remarkable results.

Representing Text as Numerical Vectors

In natural language processing (NLP), it is essential to represent text data in a numerical format that can be processed by machine learning algorithms. Word embeddings are a powerful technique for representing words as dense vectors in a continuous space. These vectors capture semantic relationships between words, allowing models to understand the meaning and context of text.

Word2Vec, GloVe, and Other Embedding Methods

Several popular methods can be used to create word embeddings:

1. Word2Vec:

Neural Network Model:

- Word2Vec is a neural network model that consists of an input layer, hidden layers, and an output layer.
- The goal of Word2Vec is to learn word embeddings that capture the semantic relationships between words. This is achieved by training the model to predict context words given a target word,

or vice versa.

Techniques:

1. **Skip-gram:**
   - **Input:** A target word.
   - **Output:** A probability distribution over context words.
   - **Training:** The model is trained to predict the surrounding context words given a target word.
   - **Intuition:** Skip-gram captures the idea that words that appear together in similar contexts are likely to have similar meanings.
2. **Continuous Bag-of-Words (CBOW):**
   - **Input:** A window of context words.
   - **Output:** A probability distribution over words.
   - **Training:** The model is trained to predict the target word given its context words.
   - **Intuition:** CBOW captures the idea that the meaning of a word is influenced by its surrounding context.

Benefits of Word2Vec:

- Semantic relationships: Word2Vec effectively captures semantic relationships between words, such as synonyms, antonyms, and analogies.
- Large datasets: Word2Vec can be trained on large datasets, allowing it to learn rich and informative word embeddings.
- Flexibility: Word2Vec can be adapted to various NLP tasks, including sentiment analysis, text classification, and machine translation.

Word2Vec is a powerful neural network-based model for learning word embeddings. By predicting context words or target words, Word2Vec captures semantic relationships between words and can be used for a wide range of NLP applications.

2. GloVe (Global Vectors for Word Representation):

Co-occurrence Statistics:

- GloVe leverages global word-word co-occurrence statistics from a large corpus of text. This means it considers how often words appear together across the entire dataset.
- A co-occurrence matrix is created, where each element represents the frequency with which two words appear together.

Matrix Factorization:

- GloVe factorizes the co-occurrence matrix to obtain word vectors. This process essentially learns the relationships between words based on their co-occurrence patterns.
- The factorization is based on a weighted least-squares model that minimizes the difference between the log-bilinear model and the actual co-occurrence probabilities.

Benefits of GloVe:

- GloVe is often faster to train than Word2Vec, especially for large datasets.
- By considering global co-occurrence statistics, GloVe captures the overall relationships between words in the corpus.
- GloVe word vectors often exhibit interesting linear substructures, making them more interpretable than some other embedding methods.
- GloVe is a popular choice for word embeddings and has been used in numerous NLP applications.

GloVe is a powerful technique for learning word embeddings that leverages global co-occurrence statistics and matrix factorization. It offers several advantages, including efficiency, interpretability, and the ability to capture global relationships between words.

3. FastText:

Character-Level Embeddings:

- FastText breaks words down into subword units (n-grams of characters) instead of treating each word as a single unit.
- This approach allows FastText to handle out-of-vocabulary words more effectively, as it can represent words based on their constituent subwords even if the entire word has not been seen during training.
- Character-level embeddings can be particularly useful for languages with complex morphology or rare words.

Subword Embeddings:

- FastText can learn subword embeddings, which capture the meaning of parts of words.
- Subword embeddings can help improve generalization to unseen words, as they can represent words based on their component parts.
- Subword embeddings are especially useful for languages with rich morphology, such as languages with inflectional or derivational affixes.

Benefits of FastText:

- FastText is more robust to out-of-vocabulary words compared to models that rely on word-level embeddings.
- Subword embeddings can improve generalization to unseen words, especially in languages with complex morphology.

- FastText is often more efficient to train than Word2Vec or GloVe, especially for large vocabularies.

FastText is a powerful technique for learning word embeddings that leverages character-level n-grams and subword embeddings. This approach can improve the model's ability to handle out-of-vocabulary words and generalize to new data, making it a valuable tool for many NLP applications.

Applications of Word Embeddings

Word embeddings have revolutionized the field of natural language processing (NLP) by providing a powerful way to represent text as numerical vectors. These embeddings capture semantic relationships between words, allowing machines to understand and process human language in a meaningful way.

Key Applications

Sentiment Analysis:

- Word embeddings can be used to determine the sentiment (positive, negative, or neutral) of a piece of text.
- Word embeddings can be used as features in a machine learning model to predict the sentiment of a text.
- Example: Classifying movie reviews as positive or negative.

Text Classification:

- Word embeddings can be used to classify text into predefined categories, such as topic, genre, or intent.
- Word embeddings can be used to create feature representations for text classification models.
- Classifying news articles into categories like politics, sports, or entertainment.

Machine Translation:

- Word embeddings can help machines understand the meaning of words and phrases in one language and translate them into another.
- Word embeddings are often used as inputs to sequence-to-sequence models, which can generate translations.
- Example: Translating English text into French.

Question Answering:

- Word embeddings can help machines understand the meaning of questions and retrieve relevant information from a given text.
- Word embeddings can capture the context of words, which is important for understanding questions and providing accurate answers.
- Answering questions about a given article or document.

Information Retrieval:

- Word embeddings can be used to measure the similarity between documents based on their semantic content.
- Search engines often use word embeddings to improve the relevance of search results.
- Retrieving relevant documents from a large corpus of text.

By effectively representing text as numerical vectors, word embeddings enable machine learning models to understand and process natural language in a meaningful way. This has led to significant advancements in various NLP tasks, and word embeddings continue to be a fundamental building block in the field.

SEQUENCE MODELS FOR TEXT DATA

Sequence models are a class of machine learning models specifically designed to handle sequential data, such as text. They capture the dependencies between elements in a sequence, allowing them to understand the context and meaning of the data.

Recurrent Neural Networks (RNNs) and Long Short-Term Memory (LSTM) Networks

RNNs: Capturing Sequential Dependencies

- RNNs have a recurrent connection that allows information to be passed from previous time steps to the current time step. This enables them to capture the context and dependencies between elements in a sequence.
- When processing a sequence, an RNN is unfolded in time, creating a network with multiple layers for each time step.
- RNNs can suffer from the vanishing gradient problem, where gradients can become very small or large during backpropagation, making it difficult to learn long-term dependencies.

LSTM: Addressing the Vanishing Gradient Problem

- LSTM networks introduce gates to control the flow of information, helping to address the vanishing gradient problem.
- **Components:** LSTMs consist of three gates:
    - Determines which information from the previous cell state should be forgotten.
    - Determines which new information should be stored in the cell state.
    - Determines which information from the cell state should be outputted.
- **Cell state:** The cell state stores information over long periods of time, allowing LSTM networks to capture long-term dependencies.

Applications in Sentiment Analysis, Text Classification, and More

Sequence models have been successfully applied to a wide range of NLP tasks, including:

- Sentiment Analysis: Determining the sentiment (positive, negative, or neutral) of a piece of text.
- Text Classification: Categorizing text into predefined categories (e.g., topic, genre, intent).
- Machine Translation: Translating text from one language to another.
- Question Answering: Answering questions based on a given text.
- Named Entity Recognition: Identifying named entities in text, such as people, organizations, and locations.
- Text Generation: Generating human-like text, such as poems, stories, or code.

Key Advantages of Sequence Models:

- Sequence models can capture the context of words and phrases in a sequence, allowing them to understand the meaning of the text.
- They can handle sequences of varying lengths, making them suitable for a wide range of NLP tasks.
- Sequence models can learn to perform complex tasks directly from raw text data, without requiring manual feature engineering.

By leveraging the power of sequence models, we can build sophisticated NLP systems that can understand and process human language in a meaningful way.

SEVEN

IMAGE AND COMPUTER VISION

Artificial intelligence, the ability to interpret and understand visual information is a crucial capability. Image and computer vision, a subfield of artificial intelligence, equips machines with the power to extract meaningful information from digital images and videos. By leveraging advanced algorithms and techniques, computer vision systems can identify objects, recognize patterns, and make intelligent decisions based on visual input. This chapter delves into the fundamental concepts, techniques, and applications of image and computer vision, empowering you to harness the potential of this transformative technology. Image and computer vision is a field of artificial intelligence that focuses on enabling computers to understand and interpret visual information from images and videos. It is a rapidly growing area with applications in various domains, from healthcare and self-driving cars to entertainment and security.

Key Concepts and Techniques:

- Image Processing: The foundation of computer vision is image processing, which involves techniques for manipulating and enhancing images. This includes tasks such as filtering, noise reduction, and feature extraction.

- Feature Extraction: Identifying and extracting meaningful features from images, such as edges, corners, and textures. These features are used to represent and analyze the visual content.
- Object Detection and Recognition: Locating and identifying objects within images or videos. This involves using techniques like region-based convolutional neural networks (R-CNN) and faster R-CNN.
- Image Segmentation: Dividing an image into different regions or segments based on their visual properties.
- Optical Flow: Analyzing the motion of objects in a sequence of images to track their movement.
- Deep Learning: Deep learning, particularly convolutional neural networks (CNNs), has revolutionized computer vision.

CNNs are highly effective at learning complex patterns and features directly from images.

IMAGE PREPROCESSING AND AUGMENTATION

Image preprocessing is the process of preparing images for analysis by applying various transformations to enhance their quality and consistency. Image augmentation is a related technique that involves creating variations of existing images to increase the dataset size and improve model generalization.

Enhancing Image Quality

- Removing noise (random variations in pixel intensity) from images to improve clarity.
- Adjusting the contrast to make features more distinguishable.
- Correcting color distortions or imbalances.
- Applying transformations such as rotation, scaling, and shearing to adjust the image's perspective or orientation.

Creating Variations

- Changing the size of the image to match the requirements of the model or to reduce computational cost.

- Extracting a portion of the image to focus on specific regions.
- Horizontally or vertically flipping the image to create variations.
- Rotating the image by a specified angle to introduce different perspectives.
- Randomly adjusting the color, brightness, and contrast of the image.
- Applying a Gaussian blur to reduce noise and smooth edges.

Benefits of Image Preprocessing and Augmentation

- Preprocessing and augmentation can help models learn more robust and generalizable features.
- Augmentation can artificially increase the size of the dataset, preventing overfitting.
- Augmentation can introduce variations in the data, making the model more resistant to changes in input conditions.
- Augmentation can act as a form of regularization, preventing the model from overfitting to the training data.

By effectively preprocessing and augmenting images, you can improve the quality and diversity of your dataset, leading to better model performance and generalization.

FEATURE EXTRACTION FROM IMAGES

Feature Extraction from Images

Feature extraction is the process of identifying and representing meaningful information from images. This information is used as input to machine learning models for tasks such as image classification, object detection, and image segmentation.

Extracting Meaningful Information from Images

Identifying Patterns:

- Feature extraction helps to identify visual cues within images that are relevant to the task at hand. For example, in object detection, features like edges, corners, and textures can be used to identify objects.

- By extracting meaningful features, we can enable machines to understand the semantic content of images, such as recognizing objects, scenes, or activities.

Reducing Dimensionality:

- Reducing the dimensionality of image data can significantly improve computational efficiency, especially for large datasets.
- High-dimensional data can lead to overfitting, where a model becomes too specialized to the training data. Feature extraction can help to mitigate this problem.
- Well-chosen features can capture the most important information in the image, while discarding redundant or irrelevant information.

Improving Model Performance:

- **Informative features:** High-quality features can provide valuable information to machine learning models, improving their accuracy and generalization.
- **Model suitability:** The choice of features should be tailored to the specific task and model being used. For example, different features may be more suitable for image classification, object detection, or image segmentation.
- **Feature engineering:** Careful feature engineering can enhance the performance of machine learning models by creating features that are more informative and relevant to the task.

By effectively extracting meaningful information from images, we can enable machines to understand and interpret visual data in a way that is similar to humans. This has led to significant advancements in various fields, including computer vision, robotics, and artificial intelligence.

Convolutional Neural Networks (CNNs) and Other Methods

Convolutional Neural Networks (CNNs)

Deep learning architecture: CNNs are a type of deep learning architecture specifically designed for processing image data. They are composed of layers that learn hierarchical features.

Convolutional layers: The core component of CNNs is the convolutional layer. It applies filters to the input image, extracting features at different levels of abstraction.

Pooling layers: Pooling layers reduce the dimensionality of the feature maps, making the network more efficient and invariant to small translations.

Fully connected layers: The final layers of a CNN are typically fully connected layers, which combine the extracted features to produce a classification or regression output.

Benefits of CNNs:

- **Automatic feature learning:** CNNs can automatically learn relevant features from raw image data without the need for manual feature engineering.
- **Hierarchical representation:** CNNs capture hierarchical features, from simple low-level features to complex high-level features.
- **Invariance to transformations:** CNNs are invariant to small translations, rotations, and scaling of the input image.

Other Feature Extraction Methods

Hand-crafted features: Traditional feature extraction techniques can still be useful in certain scenarios, especially when computational resources are limited or when domain knowledge is available.

- **SIFT (Scale-Invariant Feature Transform):**

- Invariant to scale, rotation, and illumination: SIFT detects and extracts features that are invariant to changes in scale, rotation, and illumination.

- Keypoints: SIFT identifies keypoints within an image, which are regions that are distinctive and stable under different transformations.
- Descriptors: For each keypoint, SIFT computes a 128-dimensional descriptor that captures the local image information around the keypoint.
- **SURF (Speeded-Up Robust Features):**

- Faster than SIFT: SURF is a faster version of SIFT that uses integral images for efficient computation.
- Similar properties: SURF shares many of the same properties as SIFT, including invariance to scale, rotation, and illumination.

- **HOG (Histogram of Oriented Gradients):**

- Edge orientation distribution: HOG captures the distribution of edge orientations within an image.
- Object detection: HOG is often used for object detection tasks, as it is effective at representing the shape and appearance of objects.
- Normalization: HOG features are typically normalized to make them invariant to changes in illumination and contrast.

- **Pre-trained Models**

- Time-efficient approach: Using pre-trained CNN models as feature extractors can be a time-efficient approach, especially for tasks with limited training data.
- Transfer learning: The pre-trained models can be fine-tuned on a smaller dataset to adapt to the specific task.
- Popular models: Examples of popular pre-trained CNN models include VGG, ResNet, and Inception.

Choosing the right feature extraction method depends on the specific task and the characteristics of the image data. For example, if the task requires detecting objects that are invariant to scale, rotation, and illumination, SIFT or SURF may be suitable. If the task involves recognizing patterns based on the distribution of edges and gradients, HOG may be a good choice. For complex tasks with large datasets, using pre-trained CNN models can be an effective approach. The pre-trained models can be fine-tuned on a smaller dataset to adapt to the specific task.

Choosing the Right Method:

The choice of feature extraction method depends on several factors:

- Task complexity: For complex tasks like object detection or image segmentation, CNNs are often the preferred choice.
- Dataset size: CNNs can be computationally expensive to train, so they may not be suitable for small datasets.
- Domain knowledge: If domain knowledge is available, hand-crafted features can be effective.
- Computational resources: The availability of computational resources can influence the choice of method.

By carefully considering these factors, you can select the most appropriate feature extraction method for your specific application. For complex tasks and large datasets, CNNs are often the preferred choice due to their ability to learn complex features automatically. However, hand-crafted features can still be useful in certain scenarios, especially when computational resources are limited.

APPLICATION IN IMAGE CLASSIFICATION ,OBJECT DETECTION , AND SEGMENTATION

Image Classification

Image classification is a fundamental task in computer vision that involves assigning a label or category to an image. It is a core component of many real-world applications, from object recognition to medical diagnosis.

Applications of Image Classification

Object Recognition:

- Image classification can be used to identify objects within images, such as cars, people, animals, or specific products.
- Self-driving cars, surveillance systems, visual search engines, and robotics.

Scene Classification:

- Scene classification involves categorizing images based on their overall content, such as indoor, outdoor, city, countryside, or specific scenes (e.g., kitchen, bedroom).
- : Image retrieval, content-based image search, and scene understanding for autonomous systems.

Medical Image Analysis:

- Image classification can be used to assist in diagnosing diseases based on medical images, such as X-rays, MRIs, and CT scans.
- **Applications:** Cancer detection, tumor segmentation, and other medical imaging tasks.

Other Applications:

- **Image retrieval:** Finding similar images based on their visual content.
- **Image captioning:** Generating descriptive captions for images.
- **Image quality assessment:** Evaluating the quality of images based on various metrics.

Techniques for Image Classification:

- **Convolutional Neural Networks (CNNs):** CNNs are the most commonly used approach for image classification. They are specifically designed to extract features from images and learn patterns that are relevant to the classification task.

- **Transfer learning:** Pre-trained CNN models can be fine-tuned on smaller datasets for specific image classification tasks, saving time and computational resources.
- **Ensemble methods:** Combining multiple models can improve classification accuracy and robustness.

Image classification is a versatile task with numerous applications in various domains. By leveraging advanced techniques and leveraging the power of computer vision, we can unlock new possibilities for image analysis and understanding.

Object Detection

Locating and Identifying Objects:

- Bounding boxes: Object detection involves locating objects within an image and drawing bounding boxes around them.
- Classification: The detected objects are then classified into specific categories.

Applications:

- Self-driving cars: Detecting pedestrians, traffic signs, and other vehicles is essential for autonomous navigation.
- Surveillance: Object detection can be used for surveillance purposes, such as identifying people, objects, or anomalies in video footage.
- Retail: Counting products on shelves can help optimize inventory management and prevent stockouts.
- Industrial automation: Object detection can be used for tasks such as quality control and robot guidance.

Image Segmentation

Dividing Images into Regions:

- Pixel-level classification: Image segmentation assigns a label to each pixel in an image, indicating its membership in a particular region.

- Semantic segmentation: Semantic segmentation assigns labels to objects or regions based on their semantic meaning (e.g., person, car, road).
- Instance segmentation: Instance segmentation goes a step further by identifying and segmenting individual instances of objects within an image.

Applications:

- Medical image analysis: Segmenting organs, tumors, or other structures in medical images for diagnosis and treatment planning.
- Autonomous vehicles: Understanding the scene and identifying obstacles for safe navigation.
- Robotics: Guiding robots to interact with the environment by understanding the location and properties of objects.
- Image editing: Image segmentation can be used for tasks like image editing and manipulation.

Object detection and image segmentation are essential tasks in computer vision with a wide range of applications. By leveraging advanced techniques and deep learning, we can continue to improve the accuracy and efficiency of these methods.

Advanced Techniques:

- Deep learning: Convolutional neural networks (CNNs) have revolutionized image classification, object detection, and segmentation.
- Transfer learning: Pre-trained CNN models can be fine-tuned for specific tasks, saving time and computational resources.
- Instance segmentation: Identifying and segmenting individual instances of objects within an image.

Challenges and Future Directions:

- Real-world challenges: Image and computer vision systems still face challenges in dealing with real-world conditions, such as varying lighting, occlusion, and clutter.
- Advancements in deep learning: Ongoing research is focused on developing more powerful and efficient deep learning architectures for image and computer vision tasks.
- Ethical considerations: The use of image and computer vision raises ethical concerns, such as privacy and bias.

By addressing these challenges and leveraging advanced techniques, image and computer vision will continue to play a crucial role in various industries and applications.

EIGHT

TIME SERIES DATA

Time series data is a sequence of observations or measurements collected over time, typically at regular intervals. This type of data is ubiquitous in various fields, including finance, economics, meteorology, and engineering. Analyzing time series data allows us to identify patterns, trends, and make predictions about future values.

Understanding the unique characteristics and challenges of time series data is crucial for effective analysis. Time series often exhibit patterns such as trends, seasonality, and autocorrelation, which require specialized techniques to model and forecast. By mastering the concepts and techniques of time series analysis, you can gain valuable insights from historical data and make informed decisions about future events.

TIME SERIES DECOMPOSITION

Time series decomposition is a statistical technique that involves breaking down a time series into its constituent components: trend, seasonality, and residual. This decomposition helps us better understand the underlying patterns and trends in the data, making it easier to model and forecast future values.

Components of Time Series Decomposition

Trend:

- Long-term direction: The trend captures the overall upward or downward movement in the time series over a long period.
- Examples: Increasing sales over time, decreasing unemployment rates, or rising temperatures.
- Visualization: The trend can often be visualized as a straight line or a curve that fits the overall direction of the data.

Seasonality:

- Periodic fluctuations: Seasonality refers to patterns that repeat at regular intervals, such as daily, weekly, monthly, or yearly.
- Examples: Seasonal variations in sales (e.g., higher sales during holiday seasons), temperature fluctuations, and stock market cycles.
- Visualization: Seasonal patterns can be visualized as cyclical fluctuations around the trend.

Residual:

- Random noise: The residual component represents the random fluctuations in the data that cannot be explained by the trend or seasonality.
- Noise: It often includes noise, outliers, and other irregular patterns.
- Analysis: Analyzing the residual component can help identify anomalies or unusual patterns in the data.

Decomposition Methods
Additive Decomposition:

- Sum of components: In additive decomposition, the time series is represented as the sum of the trend, seasonal, and residual components.
- Equation: Time series = Trend + Seasonality + Residual

- Suitable for: Additive decomposition is suitable when the magnitude of the seasonal component does not vary significantly with the level of the trend.

Multiplicative Decomposition:

- Product of components: In multiplicative decomposition, the time series is represented as the product of the trend, seasonal, and residual components.
- Equation: Time series = Trend * Seasonality * Residual
- Suitable for: Multiplicative decomposition is suitable when the magnitude of the seasonal component varies with the level of the trend. For example, if sales increase during a holiday season, the seasonal component might be larger for higher sales levels.

Choosing the appropriate decomposition method depends on the characteristics of the time series and the specific goals of the analysis. By understanding the components of a time series and applying appropriate decomposition techniques, we can gain valuable insights into the underlying patterns and trends in the data.

Example:

Consider a monthly sales dataset for a retail store. The trend component might show an overall increase in sales over time, while the seasonal component might capture the fluctuations in sales due to factors like holidays or weather. The residual component would represent the random variations in sales that cannot be explained by the trend or seasonality.

Benefits of Time Series Decomposition:

- **Understanding underlying patterns:** Decomposition helps identify the key drivers of the time series, making it easier to understand and interpret the data.
- **Forecasting:** By understanding the components of the time series, we can develop more accurate forecasting models.

- **Anomaly detection:** Decomposition can help identify anomalies or unusual patterns in the data.

Time series decomposition is a valuable tool for analyzing and understanding time series data. By breaking down a time series into its constituent components, we can gain valuable insights and make more informed decisions.

FEATURE ENGINEERING FOR TIME SERIES

Feature engineering plays a crucial role in time series analysis, as it involves creating new features that can capture the underlying patterns and relationships in the data. By engineering relevant features, we can improve the performance of time series models and extract valuable insights.

Creating Features: Lags, Differences, and Rolling Averages

1. **Lags:**
    - Past values: Lags are created by shifting the time series by a certain number of time steps.
    - Example: If the original time series is [1, 2, 3, 4, 5], a lag of 1 would create the new feature [0, 1, 2, 3, 4].
    - Purpose: Lags capture the dependence of current values on past values, which is common in time series data.
2. **Differences:**
    - Calculating differences: Differences are calculated by subtracting previous values from current values.
    - Example: The first difference of the time series [1, 2, 3, 4, 5] would be [1, 1, 1, 1].
    - Purpose: Differences can help to remove trends and seasonality from the data, making it easier to identify other patterns.
3. **Rolling Averages:**

  - Moving averages: Rolling averages are calculated by averaging a window of consecutive values in the time series.
  - Example: A rolling average of 3 would calculate the average of the current value and the two previous values.
  - Purpose: Rolling averages can smooth out short-term fluctuations in the data, making it easier to identify long-term trends.

Additional Features
Seasonal Differences

- Removing seasonality: Seasonal differences can be calculated by subtracting the corresponding value from the previous season. For example, to calculate the seasonal difference for April, you would subtract the April value from the previous year's April value.
- Stationarity: Creating seasonal differences can help to make the time series more stationary, which is often a requirement for many time series models.

Cycle Indicators

- Capturing periodic patterns: Cycle indicators are binary features that indicate whether a data point belongs to a specific cycle (e.g., day of the week, month, year).
- Example: For daily data, you could create features like "is_weekday," "is_weekend," and "is_holiday."
- Modeling cyclical patterns: Cycle indicators can help models capture periodic patterns that are not captured by trend or seasonality alone.

Domain-Specific Features

Leveraging domain knowledge: Domain-specific features can be created based on the unique characteristics of the data and the problem being solved.

- **Examples:**
    - In financial data, features like economic indicators, interest rates, and market sentiment can be relevant.
    - In weather data, features like temperature, humidity, and precipitation can be important.
    - In healthcare data, features like patient demographics, medical history, and treatment information can be relevant.

By creating these additional features, you can provide machine learning models with more informative inputs, improving their ability to capture the underlying patterns and make accurate predictions. The specific features that are relevant will depend on the domain and the goals of the analysis.

RECURRENT NEURAL NETWORKS (RNNs) AND LONG SHORT-TERM MEMORY (LSTM) NETWORKS

Recurrent Neural Networks (RNNs) and Long Short-Term Memory (LSTM) networks are powerful tools for modeling sequential patterns in time series data. They are specifically designed to handle sequences and capture the dependencies between elements within the sequence.

RNNs for Time Series

- **Recurrent connections:** RNNs use recurrent connections to pass information from previous time steps to the current time step, allowing them to capture the context and dependencies in the data.
- **Challenges:** RNNs can suffer from the vanishing gradient problem, which makes it difficult to learn long-term dependencies.

LSTM Networks

- **Addressing the vanishing gradient problem:** LSTMs introduce gates that control the flow of information, helping to address the vanishing gradient problem and capture long-term dependencies.

- **Components**: LSTMs consist of a forget gate, an input gate, and an output gate.
- **Cell state:** LSTMs have a cell state that stores information over time, allowing them to remember important information from previous time steps.

Applications of RNNs and LSTMs for Time Series Data

- Time series forecasting: Predicting future values of a time series based on past observations.
- Anomaly detection: Identifying unusual patterns or outliers in the data.
- Financial forecasting: Predicting stock prices, exchange rates, or other financial indicators.
- Weather forecasting: Predicting weather patterns and conditions.
- Sensor data analysis: Analyzing data from sensors to identify trends and anomalies.

By leveraging the power of RNNs and LSTMs, we can effectively model complex sequential patterns in time series data and make accurate predictions. These models are particularly well-suited for tasks that require understanding the context and dependencies between data points over time.

NINE

FEATURE ENGINEERING FOR IMBALANCED DATASETS

Imbalanced datasets, where one class significantly outnumbers the other, pose unique challenges for machine learning models. Feature engineering plays a crucial role in addressing this imbalance and improving model performance. By crafting informative features that capture the nuances of the minority class, we can enhance model sensitivity and prevent the model from being biased towards the majority class. This chapter explores effective feature engineering techniques specifically designed for imbalanced datasets, equipping you with the tools to build robust and accurate models.

CHALLENGES OF IMBALANCED DATA

Imbalanced datasets, where one class significantly outnumbers the other, pose unique challenges for machine learning models. These challenges can lead to biased models and inaccurate predictions, especially for the minority class.

Key Challenges:

1. Biased Models: Models trained on imbalanced datasets often become biased towards the majority class, leading to poor performance on the minority class. This can be particularly problematic in applications where the minority class is of greater interest, such as fraud detection or medical diagnosis.
2. Evaluation Metrics: Traditional evaluation metrics like accuracy can be misleading for imbalanced data. For example, a model that always predicts the majority class can achieve high accuracy but perform poorly on the minority class.
3. Feature Correlation: Imbalanced data can affect feature correlation and class separation, making it difficult for models to learn meaningful patterns.
4. Overfitting: Models trained on imbalanced data may be more prone to overfitting, especially if the majority class dominates the training set.
5. Sampling Bias: Sampling techniques used to handle imbalanced data can introduce bias, leading to distorted data distributions and potentially inaccurate models.

Addressing these challenges requires careful consideration of feature engineering techniques, sampling methods, and evaluation metrics. By understanding the unique challenges posed by imbalanced data, you can develop more robust and accurate models.

TECHNIQUES LIKE OVERSAMPLING , UNDERSAMPLING , AND SMOTE

Imbalanced datasets can lead to biased models that perform poorly on the minority class. To address this issue, various sampling techniques can be employed to balance the class distribution and improve model performance.

Oversampling

Increasing minority class: Oversampling involves increasing the number of instances in the minority class by creating synthetic samples or duplicating existing samples.

Techniques:

- Random oversampling: Randomly duplicating samples from the minority class.
- SMOTE (Synthetic Minority Over-sampling Technique): Generating new synthetic samples by interpolating between existing minority class samples.

Challenges: Oversampling can lead to overfitting if not done carefully.

Undersampling

Reducing majority class: Undersampling involves reducing the number of instances in the majority class.

Techniques:

- Random undersampling: Randomly removing samples from the majority class.
- Cluster-based undersampling: Clustering the majority class and selecting representative samples from each cluster.

Challenges: Undersampling can lead to loss of information and reduced model performance if not done carefully.

SMOTE (Synthetic Minority Over-sampling Technique)

Generating new samples: SMOTE generates new synthetic samples by interpolating between existing minority class samples along the lines connecting them to their nearest neighbors.

Addressing class imbalance: SMOTE effectively addresses class imbalance while preserving the distribution of the minority class.

Customization: SMOTE can be customized by adjusting parameters like the number of neighbors used for interpolation and the degree of oversampling.

Choosing the Right Technique:

The best sampling technique depends on the specific characteristics of the dataset and the desired outcome. Consider the following factors:

- Severity of imbalance: The degree of imbalance can influence the choice of technique. For severe imbalances, oversampling or SMOTE may be more effective.
- Data size: If the dataset is large, undersampling can be computationally efficient.
- Class distribution: The distribution of the minority class can also affect the choice of technique.
- Model performance: Experiment with different sampling techniques to evaluate their impact on model performance.

By carefully selecting and applying appropriate sampling techniques, you can address the challenges of imbalanced data and improve the performance of your machine learning models.

COST-SENSITIVE LEARNING AND CLASS WEIGHTING

Cost-sensitive learning is a technique used to address imbalanced datasets by assigning different costs to misclassifying different classes. This allows the model to prioritize the correct classification of the minority class, which is often more important in real-world applications.

Class weighting is a common approach to implementing cost-sensitive learning. By assigning higher weights to the minority class and lower weights to the majority class, the model is encouraged to focus on correctly classifying the minority class.

Key Considerations:

- **Cost matrix:** A cost matrix is used to define the costs associated with misclassifying each class. The higher the cost, the more important it is for the model to correctly classify that class.
- **Weighting scheme:** Different weighting schemes can be used, such as proportional weighting, inverse proportional weighting, or custom weighting based on domain knowledge.
- **Evaluation metrics:** When using cost-sensitive learning, it is important to choose evaluation metrics that are appropriate for imbalanced datasets, such as F1-score or precision-recall curve.

Benefits of Cost-Sensitive Learning:

- Improved performance on minority class: By assigning higher costs to misclassifying the minority class, cost-sensitive learning can help to improve the model's performance on this class.
- Addressing class imbalance: Cost-sensitive learning can effectively address the challenges posed by imbalanced datasets.
- Real-world applications: Cost-sensitive learning is particularly useful in applications where misclassifying certain classes has more severe consequences.

By carefully considering the costs associated with misclassification and applying appropriate weighting schemes, you can effectively address the challenges of imbalanced datasets and build more robust and accurate models.

FEATURE ENGINEERING FOR HIGH-DIMENSIONAL DATA

In the realm of machine learning, high-dimensional data, characterized by a vast number of features, presents unique challenges. The curse of dimensionality can lead to overfitting, computational inefficiencies, and degraded model performance. To overcome these obstacles, effective feature engineering techniques are essential. This chapter delves into the strategies and methodologies specifically tailored for high-dimensional data, equipping you with the tools to extract meaningful insights and build robust models.

The Curse of Dimensionality

When dealing with high-dimensional data, where the number of features is significantly large, several challenges arise:

- **Sparse data:** High-dimensional spaces tend to be sparse, meaning that data points are far apart from each other. This can make it difficult for models to learn meaningful patterns.
- **Computational complexity:** Training models on high-dimensional data can be computationally expensive, as the number of parameters increases exponentially with the number

of features.

- **Overfitting:** High-dimensional data can increase the risk of overfitting, where a model becomes too complex and learns the training data too well, leading to poor generalization.

Feature Selection and Extraction Methods

To address the curse of dimensionality, feature selection and extraction techniques can be employed to reduce the number of features while preserving relevant information.

Feature Selection:

- Filter methods: Evaluate features based on statistical measures (e.g., correlation, chi-squared test) without considering the model.
- Wrapper methods: Evaluate features based on their impact on model performance (e.g., forward selection, backward elimination).
- Embedded methods: Integrate feature selection into the model training process (e.g., L1 regularization).

Feature Extraction:

- Principal Component Analysis (PCA): Identifies the most important directions in the data (principal components) and projects the data onto a lower-dimensional space.
- t-SNE (t-Distributed Stochastic Neighbor Embedding): Preserves local structure in the data and is useful for visualization.
- Autoencoders: Neural networks trained to reconstruct input data, with the bottleneck layer acting as a dimensionality reduction technique.

Dimensionality Reduction Techniques

- Projects data onto a lower-dimensional subspace defined by the principal components, preserving the most variance.

- Preserves local structure and is suitable for visualizing high-dimensional data in a lower-dimensional space.
- Learn a compressed representation of the data through an encoder-decoder architecture.

By carefully selecting and applying feature selection and extraction techniques, you can effectively reduce the dimensionality of high-dimensional data, mitigate the curse of dimensionality, and improve the performance and interpretability of your machine learning models.

TEN

FEATURE ENGINEERING FOR CAUSALITY

In the realm of machine learning, understanding causal relationships is paramount for making informed decisions and gaining actionable insights. Feature engineering, the art of crafting meaningful features from raw data, plays a pivotal role in establishing causal connections. By carefully selecting and transforming features, we can unravel the underlying mechanisms that drive phenomena and make more accurate predictions. This chapter delves into the strategies and techniques that enable us to extract causal insights from data, empowering us to make data-driven decisions with confidence. In the dynamic field of machine learning, comprehending causal relationships is essential for making well-informed decisions and extracting actionable insights. Feature engineering, the skillful transformation of raw data into meaningful features, plays a pivotal role in establishing causal inference. By meticulously selecting and crafting features that encapsulate the underlying causal mechanisms, we can unveil the true drivers of outcomes and make more reliable predictions. This chapter delves into the strategies and techniques for feature engineering in the context of causality, empowering you to unravel intricate relationships and gain a profound understanding of your data.

THE DIFFERNCE BETWEEN CORRELATION AND CAUSATION

Correlation and causation are two terms often used interchangeably, but they have distinct meanings. Understanding the difference between these concepts is essential in data analysis and decision-making.

Correlation refers to a statistical relationship between two or more variables. When two variables are correlated, they tend to change together, but this relationship does not necessarily imply that one variable causes the other to change. In other words, correlation does not imply causation.

Causation, on the other hand, indicates a direct cause-and-effect relationship between two variables. A change in one variable directly results in a change in the other. Establishing causation is often more challenging than establishing correlation and typically requires controlled experiments or rigorous statistical methods.

Examples:

- Correlation: Ice cream sales and crime rates may be correlated, but this doesn't mean that eating ice cream causes crime. A third factor, such as warm weather, could be influencing both ice cream sales and crime rates.
- Causation: Smoking is a known cause of lung cancer. There is a strong causal relationship between smoking and the risk of developing lung cancer.

Key Points to Remember:

- Correlation does not imply causation. Just because two variables are correlated doesn't mean one causes the other.
- Establishing causation requires additional evidence. To establish causation, you often need controlled experiments, longitudinal

studies, or strong theoretical explanations.

- Confounding variables: Be aware of confounding variables, which can influence both the independent and dependent variables, leading to spurious correlations.

By understanding the difference between correlation and causation, you can avoid making incorrect conclusions and make more informed decisions based on your data analysis.

CAUSAL INFERENCE METHODS

Causal inference aims to establish causal relationships between variables, going beyond mere correlation. It involves identifying the true underlying causes of observed phenomena. Here are some common causal inference methods:

Randomized Controlled Trials (RCTs)

- Gold standard: RCTs are considered the gold standard for establishing causation.
- Randomization: Participants are randomly assigned to treatment and control groups, minimizing the influence of confounding variables.
- Controlled environment: RCTs are often conducted in controlled environments to isolate the effect of the treatment.

Observational Studies

- Real-world data: Observational studies analyze existing data without intervening in the process.
- Challenges: Establishing causation in observational studies can be challenging due to confounding variables and selection bias.
- **Methods:**
    - Matching: Matching similar individuals in the treatment and control groups to control for confounding variables.
    - Stratification: Dividing the sample into strata based on confounding variables and analyzing each stratum

separately.
  - Instrumental variables: Using an instrumental variable that is correlated with the treatment but uncorrelated with the outcome, except through its effect on the treatment.

Structural Equation Modeling (SEM)

- Graphical models: SEM uses graphical models to represent the relationships between variables.
- Causal paths: SEM can identify causal paths between variables and estimate their effects.
- Assumptions: SEM relies on assumptions about the causal structure, which may need to be validated.

Propensity Score Matching

- Balancing covariates: Propensity score matching creates matched pairs of individuals with similar probabilities of receiving the treatment.
- Controlling for confounding: This method can help control for confounding variables and improve causal inference.

Difference-in-Differences (DiD)

- Before-after comparison: DiD compares the change in an outcome variable for a treatment group and a control group before and after a treatment is implemented.
- Controlling for time trends: DiD can control for time trends that may affect both groups.

Choosing the appropriate causal inference method depends on the specific research question, the availability of data, and the feasibility of different approaches. It is often necessary to combine multiple methods and consider the limitations and assumptions associated with each. By carefully applying causal inference techniques, researchers can gain valuable insights into the underlying causes of phenomena and make more informed decisions.

APPLICATIONS OF CAUSAL INFERENCE IN MACHINE LEARNING

Causal inference is a powerful tool for understanding the underlying relationships between variables in data. It has a wide range of applications in machine learning, including:

Medical Research

- **Drug efficacy:** Evaluating the effectiveness of new drugs or treatments requires establishing a causal relationship between the drug and the outcome. Causal inference methods can help control for confounding factors and isolate the effect of the drug.
- **Disease risk factors:** Identifying the risk factors for various diseases can help develop preventive measures and targeted treatments. Causal inference can be used to establish causal relationships between risk factors and disease outcomes.
- **Personalized medicine:** By understanding the individual factors that influence disease outcomes, causal inference can help develop personalized treatment plans tailored to specific patients.

Economics

- **Policy evaluation:** Assessing the impact of government policies requires understanding the causal relationship between the policy and the outcome of interest. Causal inference methods can help isolate the effect of the policy while controlling for other factors.
- **Market analysis:** Understanding the drivers of market trends can help businesses make informed decisions. Causal inference can be used to identify the causal relationships between market factors and outcomes.

- **Causal marketing:** Evaluating the effectiveness of marketing campaigns involves understanding the causal relationship between the campaign and sales or other outcomes. Causal inference methods can help isolate the effect of the campaign and assess its return on investment.

Social Sciences

- **Social program evaluation:** Assessing the impact of social programs requires understanding the causal relationship between the program and the desired outcomes. Causal inference methods can help control for confounding factors and isolate the effect of the program.
- **Causal mediation analysis:** Causal mediation analysis can help identify the mechanisms through which interventions work. This can provide valuable insights into the underlying processes and inform future policy decisions.

Artificial Intelligence

- **Explainable AI:** Understanding why a machine learning model makes certain predictions is essential for building trust and ensuring fairness. Causal inference can help explain the underlying causal relationships that drive model predictions.
- **Fairness and bias:** Identifying and addressing biases in machine learning models is crucial for ensuring fairness and equity. Causal inference can help identify and mitigate biases by understanding the underlying causes of disparities.
- **Reinforcement learning:** Causal inference can be used to design reward functions that encourage desired behaviors in reinforcement learning agents. By understanding the causal relationships between actions and outcomes, we can create more effective reinforcement learning algorithms.

By applying causal inference techniques, machine learning models can provide more reliable and actionable insights, leading to better decision-making in various domains.

ELEVEN

FEATURE ENGINEERING FOR PRIVACY AND SECURITY

In today's data-driven world, privacy and security are paramount concerns. Feature engineering, the art of transforming raw data into meaningful features, plays a critical role in safeguarding sensitive information while preserving the utility of data for machine learning models. This chapter delves into the strategies and techniques for feature engineering that prioritize privacy and security, enabling you to build models that protect individuals' data while extracting valuable insights.

PRIVACY CONCERNS IN FEATURE ENGINEERING

Feature engineering, while crucial for machine learning, can raise significant privacy concerns. The process of transforming raw data into meaningful features can inadvertently expose sensitive information. Here are some key privacy concerns:

Data Anonymization and Pseudonymization:

- Anonymization: Removing or replacing personal identifiers (e.g., names, addresses, social security numbers) to make it impossible to identify individuals.
- Pseudonymization: Replacing personal identifiers with unique identifiers that cannot be directly linked to individuals.

Sensitive Information Leakage:

- Identifying sensitive features: Carefully assess the data to identify features that could potentially reveal sensitive information.
- Feature engineering: Modify or aggregate features to avoid revealing sensitive information while preserving the utility of the data.
- Data masking: Replace sensitive values with random or synthetic data to protect privacy.

Differential Privacy:

- Noise addition: Adding noise to the data or the model's output to make it difficult to infer individual data points.
- Privacy-utility trade-off: Balancing the need for privacy with the desire for accurate analysis.
- Differential privacy mechanisms: Techniques like Laplace noise addition or Gaussian noise addition can be used to achieve differential privacy.

Data Minimization:

- Collecting only necessary data: Collect only the data that is essential for the task at hand, avoiding unnecessary collection of personal information.
- Data retention policies: Implement policies for data retention and deletion to minimize the storage of sensitive information.

Data Security:

- Access controls: Implement strong access controls to restrict access to sensitive data.
- Encryption: Encrypt data at rest and in transit to protect it from unauthorized access.
- Regular security audits: Conduct regular security audits to identify and address vulnerabilities.

By carefully considering these privacy concerns and implementing appropriate measures, organizations can protect individuals' privacy while still deriving valuable insights from data. It is essential to strike a balance between privacy and utility, ensuring that data is used responsibly and ethically.

Addressing Privacy Concerns:

- Ethical considerations: Adhering to ethical guidelines and regulations related to data privacy and protection.
- Privacy-preserving techniques: Employing techniques like differential privacy, homomorphic encryption, and secure multi-party computation.
- Data anonymization and pseudonymization: Ensuring that personal information is anonymized or pseudonymized before feature engineering.
- Regular audits and assessments: Conducting regular audits and assessments to identify and address potential privacy risks.

By carefully considering these privacy concerns and implementing appropriate measures, we can ensure that feature engineering is conducted in a responsible and ethical manner, protecting individuals' privacy while deriving valuable insights from data.

TECHNIQUES LIKE DIFFERNTIAL PRIVACY AND ANONYMIZATON

Anonymization:

- Removing identifiers: Anonymization involves removing or replacing personal identifiers, such as names, addresses, and social security numbers, to make it difficult to identify individuals.
- Generalization: Generalizing data to a coarser level of granularity (e.g., replacing specific zip codes with broader geographic regions) can also help protect privacy.
- K-anonymization: K-anonymization ensures that each individual's data is indistinguishable from at least k other individuals in the dataset.

Comparison:

- Differential privacy: Provides a stronger guarantee of privacy by adding noise to the data, making it difficult to infer individual data points even if the entire dataset is compromised.
- Anonymization: Relies on removing or generalizing identifiers, but it may not be completely effective if additional information can be used to re-identify individuals.

Choosing the appropriate technique depends on the specific privacy requirements and the sensitivity of the data. In some cases, a combination of differential privacy and anonymization may be necessary to provide adequate privacy protection.

Considering these techniques and applying them appropriately, organizations can protect individuals' privacy while still deriving valuable insights from data.

SECURITY CONSIDERATION FOR FEATURE ENGINEERING

Feature engineering, while crucial for machine learning, can also introduce security risks if not handled carefully. Here are some key security considerations:

Data Integrity:

- Data validation: Ensure that the data used for feature engineering is accurate, complete, and free from errors or inconsistencies.

- Data quality checks: Implement data quality checks to detect and correct any anomalies or outliers.
- Data provenance: Maintain a record of the data's origin and lineage to track its history and ensure its integrity.

Feature Leakage:

Feature leakage occurs when a feature contains information that should not be known to the model during training. This can lead to biased models, compromised security, and reduced predictive performance.

Preventing Information Leakage

- Identify sensitive features: Carefully analyze the data to identify features that could reveal sensitive information, such as personal identifiers, financial data, or location data.
- Data anonymization and pseudonymization: Anonymize or pseudonymize sensitive features to protect privacy and prevent information leakage.
- Feature engineering: Modify or aggregate features to avoid revealing sensitive information while preserving the utility of the data.
- Time-based features: Avoid using features that reveal information about the future, as this can lead to data leakage and biased models.
- Cross-validation: Use proper cross-validation techniques to prevent data leakage during training and evaluation.

Examples of Feature Leakage:

- **Including the target variable in training features:** If the target variable is included in the training features, the model will have access to future information, leading to biased predictions.
- **Using features derived from future data:** Features that are calculated using future information can also lead to data

leakage.

- **Revealing sensitive information:** Features that directly or indirectly reveal sensitive information, such as personal identifiers or financial data, should be avoided.

By carefully considering these factors and taking appropriate measures, you can prevent feature leakage and ensure the security and reliability of your machine learning models.

Model Security:

Model Security is a critical aspect of deploying machine learning models in real-world applications. It involves protecting the model from various threats and ensuring its integrity and reliability.

Model Poisoning

- **Malicious data injection:** Model poisoning attacks involve injecting malicious data into the training set to influence the model's behavior.
- **Targeted attacks:** Attackers can target specific vulnerabilities in the model or training process to achieve their goals.
- **Defense mechanisms:** To protect against model poisoning, techniques like outlier detection, anomaly detection, and adversarial training can be used.

Model Theft

- **Intellectual property protection:** Model theft involves unauthorized access to or copying of a machine learning model.
- **Protection measures:** To protect against model theft, organizations can implement access controls, encryption, and watermarking techniques.
- **Model obfuscation:** Obfuscating the model's architecture or parameters can make it more difficult to reverse engineer.

Adversarial Attacks

- Manipulating inputs: Adversarial attacks involve manipulating the input data in a way that causes the model to make incorrect predictions.
- Evasion attacks: Attackers can try to evade detection by making small changes to the input data that are imperceptible to humans.
- Poisoning attacks: Adversarial attacks can also be used to poison the training data, as discussed earlier.
- Defense mechanisms: Techniques like adversarial training, input regularization, and feature randomization can help protect models against adversarial attacks.

By addressing these security threats, organizations can ensure the integrity andreliability of their machine learning models and protect their intellectual property.

Data Privacy:

- Data anonymization and pseudonymization: Ensure that personal information is anonymized or pseudonymized to protect privacy.
- Differential privacy: Consider using differential privacy techniques to add noise to the data and protect individual privacy.
- Data minimization: Collect and use only the necessary data to avoid storing unnecessary personal information.

Security Best Practices:

- Regular security audits: Conduct regular security audits to identify and address vulnerabilities.
- Access controls: Implement strong access controls to restrict access to sensitive data and systems.
- Encryption: Encrypt data at rest and in transit to protect it from unauthorized access.

- Regular updates: Keep software and systems up-to-date with the latest security patches.
- Security awareness training: Provide security awareness training to employees to help them identify and prevent security threats.

By addressing these security considerations, you can ensure that your feature engineering processes are secure and protect your data and models from potential threats.

TWELVE

FEATURE ENGINERING IN REAL-WORLD SCENARIOS

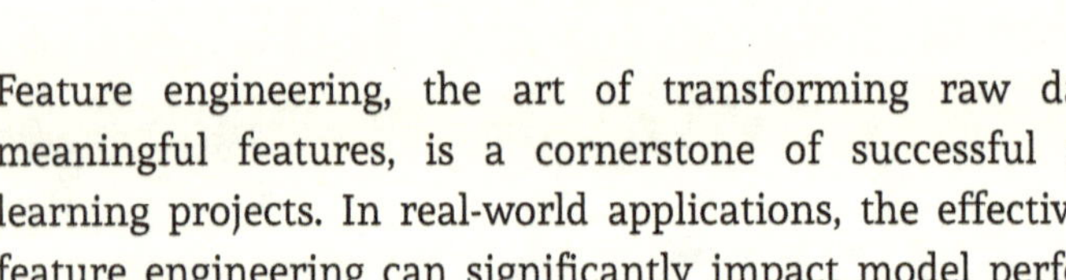

Feature engineering, the art of transforming raw data into meaningful features, is a cornerstone of successful machine learning projects. In real-world applications, the effectiveness of feature engineering can significantly impact model performance and decision-making. This chapter delves into the practical aspects of feature engineering, exploring case studies from various domains and providing insights into the challenges and best practices for crafting effective features. By understanding how feature engineering is applied in real-world scenarios, you can equip yourself with the tools to tackle complex problems and achieve exceptional results.

HEALTHCARE APPLICATIONS

Healthcare is a domain rich with data, from medical images to patient records. Effective feature engineering is crucial for extracting meaningful insights from this data and developing accurate machine learning models for various healthcare applications.

Medical Image Analysis

- Feature extraction: Extracting relevant features from medical images, such as texture, shape, and intensity patterns.
- Image preprocessing: Enhancing image quality and addressing challenges like noise, artifacts, and variations in imaging modalities.
- Deep learning: Leveraging deep learning techniques, particularly convolutional neural networks (CNNs), to automatically learn and extract features from medical images.

Patient Diagnosis

- Patient data: Combining patient demographics, medical history, symptoms, and laboratory results to create informative features.
- Time series analysis: Analyzing temporal patterns in patient data, such as changes in vital signs or medication usage.
- Feature selection: Identifying the most relevant features for predicting disease outcomes or treatment response.

Drug Discovery

- Molecular data: Engineering features from molecular structures, such as molecular descriptors, fingerprints, and similarity measures.
- Drug-target interaction prediction: Predicting the interactions between drugs and their target proteins.
- Virtual screening: Using machine learning models to identify potential drug candidates from large databases.

Challenges and Considerations:

- Data quality: Ensuring the accuracy, completeness, and consistency of healthcare data is crucial for effective feature engineering.

- Privacy and ethics: Protecting patient privacy and ensuring ethical considerations when handling sensitive healthcare data.
- Domain expertise: Collaborating with healthcare professionals to understand the domain-specific nuances and challenges.
- Interpretability: Developing models that are interpretable and can provide meaningful explanations for their predictions.

By addressing these challenges and leveraging advanced feature engineering techniques, we can harness the power of machine learning to improve healthcare outcomes and develop innovative solutions to pressing medical challenges.

FINANCIAL FORECASTING

Financial forecasting involves predicting future trends and values in financial markets. Effective feature engineering is essential for building accurate and reliable models.

Stock Price Prediction

Historical Prices:

- Past values: Using past stock prices as features can capture the underlying trends and patterns in the data.
- Lagged features: Creating lagged features (e.g., lagged returns, lagged trading volumes) to incorporate the effect of past values on future prices.
- Technical analysis: Using technical indicators derived from historical prices, such as moving averages and Bollinger Bands, to identify potential trading signals.

Technical Indicators:

- Moving averages: Calculate moving averages of different time periods to identify trends and support/resistance levels.
- Relative Strength Index (RSI): Measure the speed and change of price movements to identify overbought or oversold conditions.

- Bollinger Bands: Calculate bands around a moving average to measure volatility and identify potential price reversals.

Fundamental Factors:

- Macroeconomic factors: Consider factors like interest rates, inflation, GDP growth, and unemployment rates that can influence stock prices.
- Company financials: Analyze financial statements (e.g., income statement, balance sheet, cash flow statement) to assess the company's financial health and prospects.
- News sentiment: Extract sentiment from news articles related to the company or industry to gauge market sentiment.

Other Features:

- Volatility: Calculate volatility measures like standard deviation or variance to assess the risk associated with a stock.
- Correlation: Analyze the correlation between a stock and market indices or other related assets.
- Technical indicators: Explore other technical indicators like MACD, stochastic oscillator, and Fibonacci retracements.

By incorporating these features, you can build more informative and accurate models for stock price prediction. It is important to experiment with different feature combinations and consider the specific characteristics of the stock or market you are analyzing.

Risk Assessment

- **Risk metrics:** Engineering features related to risk, such as volatility, beta, and value at risk (VaR).
- **Creditworthiness:** For credit risk assessment, features like credit scores, debt-to-equity ratios, and payment history can be used.

Fraud Detection

- **Anomaly detection:** Creating features to identify unusual patterns or deviations from normal behavior.
- **Behavioral analytics:** Analyzing user behavior patterns to detect fraudulent activities.
- **Network analysis:** Examining relationships between entities (e.g., accounts, transactions) to identify suspicious connections.

Key Considerations:

- **Time series analysis:** Financial data is often time-series data, requiring techniques like lag features, differencing, and seasonality adjustments.
- **External factors:** Incorporating external factors such as economic indicators, news sentiment, and market events can improve model accuracy.
- **Data quality:** Ensuring data accuracy and completeness is crucial for reliable financial forecasting.
- **Model selection:** Choosing appropriate machine learning models (e.g., ARIMA, LSTM, Random Forest) based on the complexity of the problem and the characteristics of the data.

By carefully engineering features and considering these factors, you can build robust and accurate financial forecasting models.

CUSTOMER CHURN PREDICTION

Customer churn prediction is a critical task for businesses to identify customers who are likely to discontinue their services or products. Effective feature engineering plays a crucial role in building accurate models for churn prediction.

Key Features for Customer Churn Prediction

Customer Demographics:

- **Age:** Age can be a factor in customer churn, as different age groups may have different needs and preferences.

- **Gender:** Gender can also influence customer behavior and churn rates.
- **Location:** Geographic location may be relevant, especially if the company offers location-specific services or products.
- **Income level:** Income level can be a factor in customer churn, as higher-income customers may be more likely to afford premium services.
- **Tenure with the company:** Customers who have been with the company for a longer period of time may be less likely to churn.

Customer Behavior:

- **Purchase frequency:** Customers who purchase frequently are more likely to be engaged and less likely to churn.
- **Purchase amount:** Customers who make larger purchases may be more valuable to the company and less likely to churn.
- **Product usage:** The level of product usage can be a good indicator of customer satisfaction and engagement.
- **Customer support interactions:** Frequent or negative customer support interactions can be a sign of dissatisfaction and increased churn risk.
- **Social media engagement:** Engagement on social media can be a measure of customer satisfaction and loyalty.

Contractual Information:

- **Contract type:** The type of contract (e.g., monthly, annual) can influence churn rates.
- **Contract length:** Longer-term contracts may be associated with lower churn rates.
- **Renewal status:** Customers who have recently renewed their contracts are less likely to churn.

Payment History:

- **Payment frequency:** Customers who pay on time are less likely to churn.
- **Payment delays:** Late or missed payments can be a sign of financial difficulties and increased churn risk.
- **Payment method:** The payment method (e.g., credit card, direct debit) may be relevant, especially if there are issues with payment processing.

Churn Indicators:

- **Recent service cancellations:** Customers who have recently canceled services or downgraded their plans are more likely to churn.
- **Complaints:** Customers who have filed complaints or expressed dissatisfaction may be at a higher risk of churning.

By carefully considering these features and their relevance to your specific business, you can build more accurate models for customer churn prediction and take proactive steps to retain your valuable customers.

Feature Engineering Techniques

- **Time-based features:** Create features based on time-related information, such as time since last purchase, days since last login, or months since contract renewal.
- **Recency, Frequency, Monetary (RFM) analysis:** Calculate RFM scores to assess customer value and identify potential churners.
- **Customer lifetime value (CLTV):** Estimate the future value of a customer to prioritize retention efforts.
- **Sentiment analysis:** Analyze customer feedback (e.g., reviews, social media posts) to gauge customer satisfaction.
- **Clustering:** Group customers based on similar characteristics to identify distinct segments with different churn rates.

Challenges and Considerations

- Data quality: Ensure the accuracy and completeness of customer data.
- Feature relevance: Select features that are most relevant to churn prediction and avoid including irrelevant or redundant features.
- Imbalanced data: Address class imbalance (where churn is a minority class) using techniques like oversampling, undersampling, or class weighting.
- Model selection: Choose appropriate machine learning models (e.g., logistic regression, random forest, XGBoost) based on the characteristics of the data and the complexity of the problem.

By carefully engineering features and considering these factors, you can build accurate models for customer churn prediction and take proactive steps to retain valuable customers.

OTHER APPLICATION

Feature engineering is a versatile technique that can be applied to a wide range of industries and applications. Here are some examples from various domains:

1. Retail

Customer Segmentation:

- Demographic features: Age, gender, location, income level
- Purchase behavior features: Purchase frequency, purchase amount, product categories, recency of purchase
- Customer lifetime value (CLTV): Calculate CLTV based on customer spending patterns and retention rates.

Product Recommendation:

- Collaborative filtering: Use similarity measures between customers or products to recommend items.
- Content-based filtering: Recommend products based on their attributes (e.g., brand, category, price).
- Hybrid approaches: Combine collaborative filtering and content-based filtering for more accurate recommendations.

Churn Prediction:

- Identify at-risk customers: Use features such as purchase frequency, recent purchases, and customer support interactions to predict churn.
- Implement retention strategies: Develop targeted retention campaigns to address the needs of at-risk customers.

2. Manufacturing

Predictive Maintenance:

- Sensor data: Collect data from sensors on equipment to monitor its performance and identify potential failures.
- Time series analysis: Use time series analysis techniques to identify patterns and trends in sensor data.
- Machine learning models: Train machine learning models to predict equipment failures based on sensor data and historical maintenance records.

Quality Control:

- Image analysis: Use computer vision techniques to inspect products for defects.
- Sensor data: Analyze sensor data from manufacturing processes to identify quality issues.
- Statistical analysis: Use statistical methods to assess product quality and identify outliers.

Supply Chain Optimization:

- Inventory management: Optimize inventory levels using demand forecasting and inventory optimization techniques.
- Transportation optimization: Optimize transportation routes and schedules to reduce costs and improve efficiency.

- Production planning: Optimize production schedules based on demand forecasts and resource availability.

3. Marketing

Customer Segmentation:

- RFM analysis: Use recency, frequency, and monetary value to segment customers based on their purchasing behavior.
- Demographic segmentation: Segment customers based on age, gender, location, and other demographic factors.
- Psychographic segmentation: Segment customers based on their lifestyle, values, and interests.

CLTV Prediction:

- Estimate the future value of customers based on their purchase history, demographics, and behavior.
- Prioritize retention efforts for high-value customers.

Campaign Optimization:

- **A/B testing:** Test different marketing campaigns to identify the most effective ones.
- **Personalization:** Tailor marketing messages to individual customers based on their preferences and behavior.
- **Channel optimization:** Determine the most effective marketing channels for reaching the target audience.

These industries, businesses can gain valuable insights, optimize operations, and improve customer satisfaction.

Additional Industries

- **Finance:** Predicting stock prices, credit risk, and fraud.
- **Healthcare:** Predicting disease outcomes, optimizing treatment plans, and analyzing medical images.

- **Energy:** Forecasting energy consumption and demand.
- **Transportation:** Optimizing transportation routes and schedules.

By applying feature engineering techniques to these and other industries, businesses can gain valuable insights, improve decision-making, andoptimize their operations. The specific features that are relevant will vary depending on the domain and the specific problem being addressed.

THIRTEEN
EMERGING TRENDS AND FUTURE DIRECTIONS

As machine learning continues to evolve, so too does the field of feature engineering. Staying abreast of emerging trends and future directions is essential for maximizing the potential of your models. This chapter explores the latest developments in feature engineering, including automated techniques, explainable AI, and domain-specific approaches. By understanding these trends, you can equip yourself with the tools to tackle future challenges and stay at the forefront of the field. As machine learning continues to advance, feature engineering will remain a critical component of successful model development. By staying informed about emerging trends and techniques, you can ensure that your models are equipped to handle the challenges of modern data-driven applications.

AUTOMATED FEATURES ENGINEERING

Automated feature engineering is revolutionizing the way we approach building machine learning models. By automating the process of creating and selecting relevant features, it significantly reduces the time and effort required, especially for large and complex datasets. Let's delve deeper into the tools and techniques that power this exciting field.

AutoML Platforms:

Imagine a machine learning platform that not only trains models but also crafts high-performing features! AutoML platforms like Auto-Keras, H2O.ai, and TPOT do just that. They can automatically:

- **Generate different feature combinations:** These platforms explore various ways to combine existing features, creating a pool of potential candidates.
- **Evaluate feature combinations:** They assess the performance of each combination (e.g., using accuracy or other metrics) to identify the most effective ones.

Feature Selection Algorithms:

Not all features are created equal. Feature selection algorithms automatically identify the most relevant features that contribute significantly to model performance. Some common methods include:

- **Recursive Feature Elimination (RFE):** This technique iteratively removes the least important feature and repeats the process until a desired number of features remain.
- **Correlation Analysis:** It measures the strength of the relationship between features and the target variable. Features with high correlation to the target are often considered valuable.
- **Feature Importance Scores:** Machine learning models themselves can provide insights into feature importance. These scores indicate how much a particular feature influences the model's predictions.

Feature Generation Techniques:

Automated feature engineering goes beyond picking existing features; it can also create new ones! Here are some common techniques:

- **Polynomial Features:** Imagine squaring a feature or multiplying two features. These are examples of polynomial features, which can capture complex relationships between existing features.
- **Interaction Features:** Sometimes, the product or quotient of two features holds more significance than the individual features themselves. Interaction features explore these relationships.
- **Time Series Features:** For data collected over time, automated techniques can create features like lags (past values), differences (changes over time), and rolling averages (smoothed trends).
- **Domain-Specific Features:** Domain knowledge can be crucial. Automated tools can be tailored to specific domains (e.g., finance, healthcare) to generate relevant features based on domain expertise.

Beyond the Basics:

- **Genetic Algorithms:** Inspired by natural selection, genetic algorithms mimic evolution to find the optimal set of features. They iteratively combine, mutate, and select feature combinations to arrive at the "fittest" ones.
- **Neural Networks:** Deep learning models act as powerful feature extractors. By learning from raw data, they can automatically capture complex and hierarchical features, often eliminating the need for manual feature engineering altogether.

The Benefits of Automation:

- **Reduced Manual Effort:** Automating feature engineering saves valuable time and resources, especially for complex datasets.
- **Improved Efficiency:** Automated techniques can explore a vast space of feature combinations more efficiently than manual methods.

- **Increased Objectivity:** Removing human bias from feature selection can lead to more robust models.
- **Handling Complex Data:** Automated techniques can deal with complex data types and relationships that might be challenging to capture manually.

A Word of Caution:

While automated feature engineering offers significant advantages, it's not a magic bullet. Human expertise remains crucial for:

- **Domain Knowledge:** Understanding the underlying problem and data is essential to guide the automation process and select the most appropriate techniques.
- **Evaluation and Refinement:** Even with automation, evaluating the generated features and making necessary adjustments is vital for optimal performance.

By combining human expertise with the power of automation, we can unlock the full potential of feature engineering and build even more powerful machine learning models.

Benefits of Automated Feature Engineering

- Automated feature engineering can significantly reduce the time and effort required for feature engineering, especially for large and complex datasets.
- Automated techniques can efficiently explore different feature combinations and select the most relevant ones.
- Automated feature selection can help to reduce bias and subjectivity in the feature engineering process.
- Automated techniques can handle complex data types and relationships that would be difficult to engineer manually.

While automated feature engineering can be a valuable tool, it is important to note that it is not a complete replacement for human expertise. Domain knowledge and careful evaluation are still essential for ensuring the quality and relevance of the generated features.

EXPLAINABLE AI AND FEATURE ATTRIBUTION

Explainable AI (XAI) is a growing field that focuses on making machine learning models more transparent and interpretable. One key aspect of XAI is understanding the importance of individual features in a model's decision-making process. This is known as feature attribution.

The Importance of Feature Attribution

- **Understanding model decisions:** Feature attribution helps us understand how a model arrives at its predictions. This can be crucial for gaining insights into the underlying patterns and relationships in the data.
- **Building trust:** By understanding why a model makes certain decisions, we can build trust in the model and its outputs.
- **Identifying biases:** Feature attribution can help identify potential biases in the data or model, ensuring fairness and equity.
- **Improving model performance:** Understanding the importance of features can guide feature engineering and model refinement to improve performance.

Feature Attribution Methods

Feature attribution techniques help us understand how individual features contribute to a model's predictions. This information can be valuable for interpreting model behavior, identifying biases, and improving model performance.

SHAP (SHapley Additive exPlanations)

- Game theory: SHAP is based on game theory, specifically the Shapley value concept.
- Feature contributions: SHAP calculates the contribution of each feature to the final prediction by considering all possible

coalitions of features.

- Global and local explanations: SHAP can provide both global and local explanations. Global explanations show the overall importance of features, while local explanations show the importance of features for a specific prediction.

LIME (Local Interpretable Model-Agnostic Explanations)

- Local approximation: LIME approximates the complex model with a simpler, more interpretable model (e.g., a linear model) locally around a specific prediction.
- Feature importance: The coefficients of the simpler model can be used to assess the importance of features in the local region.
- Model-agnostic: LIME is applicable to a wide range of machine learning models, regardless of their complexity.

Permutation Importance

- Random permutation: Permutation importance measures the importance of a feature by randomly permuting its values and observing the impact on the model's performance.
- Feature importance: The change in performance indicates the importance of the feature.
- Simple to implement: Permutation importance is a simple and intuitive method to assess feature importance.

Partial Dependence Plots

- Visualizing feature relationships: Partial dependence plots visualize the relationship between a feature and the predicted outcome, while controlling for the effects of other features.
- Understanding feature impact: By examining the shape of the plot, we can understand how changes in the feature affect the prediction.

- Identifying non-linear relationships: Partial dependence plots can reveal non-linear relationships between features and the predicted outcome.

By using these feature attribution methods, we can gain valuable insights into the factors that drive model predictions and improve our understanding of the underlying relationships in the data.

Applications of Feature Attribution

Feature attribution is a valuable tool for understanding the factors that drive model predictions in various domains. Here are some specific applications:

Medical Diagnosis

- Understanding disease factors: By identifying the key features that contribute to a disease diagnosis, medical professionals can gain insights into the underlying causes and develop more effective treatments.
- Improving diagnostic accuracy: Feature attribution can help identify biases in the data or model, leading to more accurate and equitable diagnoses.
- Explanation to patients: Explaining the factors that contributed to a diagnosis can help patients understand their condition and treatment options.

Financial Risk Assessment

- Identifying risk factors: Feature attribution can help identify the factors that contribute to credit risk, such as income, debt-to-income ratio, and payment history.
- Improving lending decisions: By understanding these factors, financial institutions can make more informed decisions about loan approval and risk management.
- Explaining credit decisions: Explaining the factors that influenced a credit decision can help build trust with customers.

Fraud Detection

- Understanding fraudulent patterns: Feature attribution can help identify the features that are indicative of fraudulent activity, such as unusual transaction patterns or suspicious behavior.
- Preventing fraud: By understanding these patterns, organizations can develop more effective fraud detection systems and take proactive measures to prevent fraud.
- Explaining fraud alerts: Explaining the reasons for a fraud alert can help build trust with customers and reduce false positives.

In addition to these examples, feature attribution can be applied to a wide range of other domains, such as marketing, customer service, and natural language processing. By understanding the importance of features in model decisions, we can gain valuable insights, build trust, and ensure that models are making fair and equitable predictions.

FEATURE ENGINEERING FOR FEDERATED LEARNING

Federated learning is a machine learning paradigm where multiple clients (e.g., devices, organizations) collaboratively train a shared model without sharing their raw data. This approach preserves data privacy while allowing for the development of powerful models.

Feature engineering plays a crucial role in federated learning, as it can significantly impact model performance and privacy preservation. By carefully selecting and engineering features, we can extract valuable information from the distributed data while minimizing the risk of privacy breaches.

Key Considerations for Feature Engineering in Federated Learning

Data Heterogeneity:

- **Different distributions:** Federated learning often involves data from multiple sources, which may have different distributions and characteristics. This can make it challenging to extract meaningful features that are applicable across all clients.

- **Robust feature engineering:** Feature engineering techniques should be robust to data heterogeneity, ensuring that they can extract relevant information from diverse datasets.
- **Normalization and standardization:** Techniques like normalization and standardization can help to mitigate the effects of data heterogeneity by ensuring that features are on a similar scale.

Privacy Preservation:

- **Sensitive information:** Federated learning aims to train a model without sharing raw data, which is crucial for protecting privacy.
- **Feature engineering techniques:** Feature engineering techniques should avoid revealing sensitive information about the data. For example, using anonymized or aggregated features can help protect privacy.
- **Differential privacy:** Adding noise to the data or features can introduce randomness, making it more difficult to infer sensitive information from the model.

Communication Efficiency:

- **Reducing data transmission:** Feature engineering can help reduce the amount of data that needs to be transmitted between clients and the central server.
- **Feature selection:** Selecting the most relevant features can reduce the dimensionality of the data, leading to smaller model updates and faster communication.
- **Compression:** Compressing the features can also help reduce communication overhead.

Model Performance:

- **Relevant features:** Selecting features that are relevant to the task at hand is crucial for model performance.
- **Feature engineering techniques:** Careful feature engineering can improve the quality and informativeness of the features, leading to better model performance.
- **Model evaluation:** Evaluating the performance of the model on different subsets of the data can help identify the most effective features.

By carefully considering these factors and applying appropriate feature engineering techniques, we can effectively leverage federated learning to train powerful models while preserving data privacy and ensuring good model performance.

Feature Engineering Techniques for Federated Learning

Local Feature Engineering:

- Data privacy: Performing feature engineering locally on each client's device helps to protect sensitive data from being shared with a central server.
- Reduced communication: Local feature engineering can reduce the amount of data that needs to be transmitted between clients and the central server, improving communication efficiency.
- Customization: Clients can tailor their feature engineering techniques to their specific data and requirements.

Homomorphic Encryption:

- Encrypted computations: Homomorphic encryption allows for computations to be performed on encrypted data without decrypting it.
- Privacy preservation: By using homomorphic encryption, clients can share encrypted features with the central server, preserving the privacy of their data.
- Model training: The central server can train the model on the encrypted features, ensuring that the model learns from the

combined data without revealing sensitive information.

Differential Privacy:

- Noise addition: Differential privacy involves adding noise to the data or features to make it more difficult to identify individual data points.
- Privacy protection: This technique helps to protect the privacy of individual clients while still allowing for meaningful model training.
- Trade-off between privacy and accuracy: The amount of noise added must be carefully balanced to ensure that the model can still learn from the data.

Federated Averaging:

- Model aggregation: Federated averaging involves the central server averaging the updated model parameters from different clients. This ensures that the model learns from the combined data without sharing raw data.
- Privacy preservation: Federated averaging helps to protect the privacy of individual clients by aggregating the model updates rather than sharing raw data.
- Efficiency: Federated averaging can be more efficient than traditional centralized training, as it reduces the need to transmit large amounts of data.

By carefully considering these techniques and applying them appropriately, we can effectively leverage federated learning to train powerful models while preserving data privacy and ensuring good model performance.These factors and applying appropriate feature engineering techniques, we can effectively leverage federated learning to train powerful models while preserving data privacy.

FOURTEEN
CONCLUSION

In this book, we have embarked on a journey to unlock the hidden patterns within data through the power of advanced feature engineering. We have explored a wide range of techniques, from traditional methods to cutting-edge approaches, equipping you with the tools to transform raw data into valuable insights. By mastering advanced feature engineering, you can elevate your machine learning models, achieve exceptional results, and drive innovation in your domain. Remember, the art of feature engineering is a continuous process of experimentation, refinement, and adaptation. As the field of machine learning evolves, so too will the techniques for extracting meaningful information from data. By staying curious and embracing new methodologies, you can unlock the full potential of your models and make a lasting impact. This book has delved into the intricate world of advanced feature engineering, a fundamental aspect of successful machine learning projects. By mastering the techniques presented, you've equipped yourself with the tools to uncover hidden patterns, elevate model performance, and drive innovation across diverse domains. From automating feature generation to ensuring model interpretability, the field of feature engineering is continually evolving, offering exciting avenues for exploration and advancement. As you continue your machine learning journey, remember that feature engineering is an ongoing pursuit, demanding a blend of creativity, domain expertise, and technical proficiency. By embracing the challenges and seizing the opportunities that lie ahead, you can push the boundaries of what's possible and achieve remarkable outcomes in your endeavors. As machine learning continues to evolve, so too does the field of feature engineering. Here are some emerging trends and potential future directions .GANs can be used to generate synthetic data, which can be used for feature engineering and data augmentation. NAS can automatically search for the optimal architecture and feature engineering techniques for a given task. XAI techniques can help us understand the importance of different features in a model's predictions. XAI can help identify biases in the data or model, which can be addressed through feature engineering. Developing feature engineering techniques that are tailored to specific industries, such as healthcare, finance, or manufacturing. Working closely with domain experts to identify relevant features and avoid biases. Developing feature engineering techniques that preserve privacy while enabling effective model training in federated learning environments. Addressing the challenges of feature engineering in federated learning, where data may be distributed across multiple devices or organizations. Exploring new deep learning architectures for time series feature engineering, such as temporal convolutional networks (TCNs) and recurrent neural networks with attention mechanisms. techniques to capture long-term dependencies in time series data, which can be challenging for traditional feature engineering methods.

As machine learning continues to advance, feature engineering will remain a crucial component of successful model development. By staying informed about emerging trends and techniques, you can ensure that your models are equipped to handle the challenges of future applications. Exploring these advanced feature engineering techniques, you can unlock the full potential of your machine learning models and achieve even better results

www.ingramcontent.com/pod-product-compliance
Lightning Source LLC
LaVergne TN
LVHW091106150826
845673LV00002B/738

9798895888209